CYCLING

14 Legendary Riders
14 Unforgettable Feats

GRAHAM ADIN

Foreword

The rich and captivating history of cycling is built on the cumulative careers of riders, from the most humble to the greatest champions. Their journeys are marked by victories, glory, remarkable feats, strokes of luck both good and bad, seized or missed opportunities, tough breaks, and descents into hell.

Together, we will revisit the careers of the greatest cyclists of all time, focusing on their major accomplishments. As you turn these pages, you will uncover the challenges they overcame and the sacrifices they made. These Giants of the road, each in their own way, have left an indelible mark on the history of this sport, pushing the boundaries of endurance, skill, and determination.

The 14 narratives in this book, each representing an exceptional sporting destiny, can be read in any order. Every tale is unique, as each champion embodies a different aspect of the world of the "little queen".

The bidons are filled, the gears are oiled, and the feet are set... we are ready to embark on a journey through the ages. Follow my lead to experience the adrenaline of every sprint, the tension of the climbs, and the indescribable thrill of crossing the finish line as a victor!

This work is the result of extensive research and cross-referencing of various sources. As I like to say, credit must be given where credit is due. I would like to acknowledge the meticulous work of certain sources and thank the authors of all the documentation used to compile this book.

42krunning.com
Agoravox.fr
Austade.fr
Bikes.kleta.com
Cyclingheroes.com
Cyclingranking.com
Cyclingweekly.com
Cyclingmagazine.ca
Cyclist.co.uk
Dhnet.be
Dicodusport.fr
Eurosport.fr
Fatnick.com
Forum.velo-club.net
Histoire générale de la vélocipédie
Hunger
Ilciclismo.it
Lagrandeboucle.com
Ledicodutour.com
Legenducyclisme.com
Lepetitbraquet.fr
Les-sports.info
Letemps.ch
Memoire-du-cyclisme.eu

Nous étions jeunes et insouciants
Ouest-France
Proximus.be
Rtbf.be
TF1info.fr
Topvelo.fr
Trackpiste.com
Treccani.it
Velo101.com
Velofute.com
Velopack.fr
Veloptimum.net
Westsuffolkwheelers.org

CONTENTS

Foreword .... *III*

1 – "A Man Alone in Command": Fausto Coppi 1

2 – High-Powered German Machine: Jan Ullrich 11

3 – The Cannibal and The Old Lady: Eddy Merckx 19

4 – Time Trials and Records: Chris Boardman 35

5 – Fortune and Misfortune of A Scholar: Laurent Fignon 51

6 – And For A Few Seconds More: Greg LeMond 65

7 – The Lady on The Bicycle: Beryl Burton 79

8 – Against All Odds: Freddy Maertens 91

9 – The Irish Descent: Sean Kelly 109

10 – In The Shadow of A Giant: Felice Gimondi 115

11 – The Legend of The Green Giant: Erik Zabel 129

12 – The Eagle of The Mountains: Federico Bahamontes 141

13 – The Flying Parisian: James Moore 157

14 – Return To The Summit: Alberto Contador 169

1

"A Man Alone in Command": Fausto Coppi

In 1949, Italy was still healing from the scars of World War II and rebuilding itself. That year, the Giro d'Italia, Italy's grand tour, kicked off from Sicily, making its way up the peninsula.

Until the 8th stage, the pink jersey of the leader was alternately worn by Mario Fazio and Giordano Cottur. Then, during the 9th stage, Adolfo Leoni seized the first place, settling into the top spot for the following seven days.

Leoni fought tooth and nail to keep the pink jersey for as long as possible; to lead for just one more day. As the peloton faced daunting alpine summits ahead, the leader's position became decidedly uncomfortable. Leoni's closest rivals in the general classification were breathing down his neck. The Legnano sprinter harbored no illusions...

On the morning of June 10, 1949, at the start of the 17th stage from Cuneo to Pinerolo, Fausto Coppi, second, needed to pull back 43 seconds to get the first position. Gino Bartali, his eternal rival, was third, nearly 9 minutes behind.

Despite his resolve to push hard on the pedals, even to the point of bursting his thighs if necessary, Leoni knew his moments in pink were numbered. Coppi, known for his "effortless" climbing, only needed to manage the day's route well to take over the lead.

To a lesser extent, Bartali, racing for his namesake team, could also surprise. True, 9 minutes is a huge gap, but mountain stages can overturn certainties. And with the added possibility of mechanical failures, the impossible becomes possible.

So, mountains were on the agenda for the day. A lot of mountains. Terrible slopes. Summits already legendary at the time, lining up like links in a chain. The Giro riders set off from Cuneo to reach Pinerolo, traversing a route through the French Queyras. A whopping 254 kilometers with five major grunts to conquer, including the Madeleine, Vars, Izoard, Montgenèvre, and Sestrière.

The peloton started at a pace manageable for all, with Coppi and Bartali leading. They watched each other closely, each ready to accelerate at the slightest movement from the other. Coppi stuck to his favorite teammate from Bianchi, Andrea Carrea, a tough and gritty rouleur who fervently cleared the path for him.

The initial climbs were tackled with little difficulty. As the Madeleine loomed, rain joined the fray. Near Argentera, Coppi noticed an issue with his chain. Carrea attempted to oil it while pedaling standing up, a maneuver too risky and ineffective. The Bianchi duo decided to stop briefly to oil the mechanism.

Seizing the moment, Primo Volpi from Arbos launched an attack. Seeing this, Coppi mounted his bike in a flash and chased after him. A group of about ten riders, including Astrua, Martini, Cottur, and Bresci, followed suit. Gino Bartali watched the breakaways helplessly, struggling with a faulty brake cable. He eventually fixed it and launched a solo chase.

At the front, Fausto Coppi quickly caught up with Volpi, effortlessly overtaking and distancing him. After a turn, Coppi vanished from Volpi's view. When Volpi completed the turn, he found Coppi far ahead, maintaining an incredible cadence.

As the lone leader reached the midpoint of the Madeleine climb, the rain stopped. The paved road gave way to a muddy, narrow, steep, and winding path. In the post-war years, the main communication routes were prioritized for rehabilitation, neglecting mountain roads, which were poorly maintained, causing suffering for both riders and their bikes.

By then, Volpi, in second place, was already 1'30" behind. The chasing group, which Bartali had joined, was about 2'15" back. Leoni, more than 3 minutes behind, was effectively dethroned.

Coppi then made a swift and smooth descent, showcasing his skill in controlling his bike under difficult conditions. He reached the village of Gleizolles in no time, with the Col de Vars next in line.

Though he could have just maintained his pace, the lead rider did not ease his effort. He powered up the Vars slopes like a motorbike. Behind him, with a significant delay, Gino Bartali felt the need to prove something. He sprinted on the initial slopes of the climb. Primo Volpi, responsive, followed him, but they couldn't close the gap. Worse, it widened minute by minute. Bartali reached the top of Vars alone, 4'30" behind, as Volpi dropped back due to a chain issue.

The race's highest point, the Izoard, was next. The Bianchi rider continued to exert extraordinary power. Writer and artist Dino Buzzati, covering the race as a reporter, was astounded by the performance, noting, "One could see the muscles, under the skin, resembling extraordinarily young snakes, as if they were just unpacked."

As Bartali began the Izoard descent, Coppi was 6'55" ahead. The third rider, Jomaux, was 10'40" behind.

Montgenèvre, marking the return to Italy, was merely a formality. To ease saddle soreness, Fausto periodically stood up to pedal, his long legs conveying a surprising sense of lightness. Then he sat back down and resumed his relentless pace.

In the day's final climb, Sestrière, Gino Bartali, though powerless in what could be called a long-distance duel, remained determined. Fate, however, would signal that it was decidedly not on his side that June 10th.

Spectators along the road cheered for the chaser. Some threw bouquets of flowers, a kind gesture. But as the saying goes, the road to hell is paved with good intentions.

By accident, a bouquet got caught between the chain and the crankset, and the metal wire binding the flower stems jammed in the unfortunate Gino's derailleur. It took nearly four long minutes to get his bike back in working order.

Before the race, Bianchi's team manager Giovanni Tragella had asked Coppi for a list of supplies for his feed zones. "Bread, salami, and lights!"

was his rider's reply. A stylish way to tell Tragella that the day would be long, tough, but he would see it through no matter what.

The climber, unleashed, wouldn't need the lights he'd requested. He crossed the finish line while the sun was still high, exhausted, his face covered in a mask of mud, after a 192-kilometer solo breakaway. An incredible feat! He could have just made up the time needed to catch Leoni and managed his lead. Instead, he gifted the Giro with a moment that would go down in history.

Bartali finished in Pinerolo 11 minutes and 52 seconds behind his rival. Martini, the third-place rider, arrived almost 8 minutes later.

The Piedmontese's performance stunned everyone, from casual spectators to seasoned cycling observers. It was during this stage that the famous Italian journalist Mario Ferretti, covering the event, uttered the now-legendary phrase: "One man leads, his shirt is blue and white, his name is Fausto Coppi."

After his remarkable performance, Fausto Coppi retained the "maglia rosa" the following day. The day after that, June 12, he was triumphantly crowned at the Monza autodrome, where the 1949 Giro concluded.

That same year, he also won the Tour de France, becoming the first to achieve the Giro-Tour double. His pedaling style became legendary, and his reputation reached the heights of the famous Eddy Merckx. Some argue that the Italian cannot be compared to the Belgian champion, while others believe that his personal and sporting journey was far more tumultuous, thus he should be considered superior.

Born in Castellania, Piedmont, Fausto began cycling daily in his pre-teens to get to the butcher shop where he worked. Whenever he had the chance, he would ride his bike around the local roads, just for the joy of it.

In 1937, he won his first amateur race. He loved the effort involved and dreamed of becoming a professional cyclist.

A customer of the butcher shop where he worked was none other than Biagio Cavanna, known as Il Cieco (The Blind Man) due to his blindness. Cavanna was a renowned sports masseur. He took Fausto under his wing and introduced him to the sports director of the Legnano professional team.

Coppi was already an outstanding climber and a remarkable rouleur. Through solo breakaways that would become legendary, Coppi clinched his first Giro in 1940, at just 20 years old, becoming the youngest rider to win the competition. It was also during this time that his rivalry with Gino Bartali began, which would only grow over the years.

With Europe in turmoil and the Giro d'Italia not being contested, Fausto had to "settle" for winning smaller races in 1941, such as the Tours of Tuscany, Veneto, and Emilia.

In November 1942, he broke the hour record, previously held by Maurice Archambaud. Then, caught up in the war, he was drafted into the Italian army. Sent to combat in Tunisia in March 1943, he was taken prisoner by British troops.

Released at the end of the conflict, the promising Coppi was a shadow of his former self. Rumors spread that he was lost to cycling. Suffering from malnutrition and ravaged by malaria, he was so emaciated that there were fears for his life.

Armed with an iron will, he fought back, making superhuman efforts. His mentor-guru played a crucial role in his recovery. Il Cecio supported him at every moment and used his own "particular" method, emphasizing the intensity of training sessions over their duration. This was the precursor to interval training.

An innovative diet, based on wheat germ and white meat, devised by the soon-to-be-famous nutritionist Gaylord Hauser, complemented this. Nutrition would remain one of Coppi's battle horses throughout his career. He continued to work closely with the medical community to gauge the impact of his diet on his performances.

Curious by nature, Fausto also took a keen interest in bicycle mechanics. He saw it as an excellent way to amplify his natural athletic abilities. He became the first to use lighter bikes in time trials.

After his convalescence, Coppi made a sensational return to competition. He won the 1946 Milan-San Remo with Bianchi, pulling off one of his greatest feats: a 270 km breakaway, 140 km of which were solo!

Then the victories began to pile up, including, among the most prestigious, a Giro in 1947, and two Giro-Tour doubles in 1949 and 1952.

Soaring from Grand Tour victories to classic wins (three Milan-San Remos, one Paris-Roubaix, one Flèche Wallonne, and five Tours of Lombardy adorn his trophy gallery), nothing seemed to stop him. His fiery legs propelled him ever faster, ever stronger. His atypical physique gave him a much larger lung capacity than average, making him unbeatable in mountain stages and allowing him to achieve extraordinary performances on the track and in time trials. He kept his pursuers far behind him. Until 1954, he was, so to speak, never caught during his breakaways.

Throughout these years, his constant sporting rivalry with Bartali became a thrilling sports saga. Unfortunately for poor Gino, he often had to settle for second place. Over time, their sports adversarial relationship, often magnified by a sales-hungry press, gave way to a genuine and strong friendship.

In 1953, Coppi reached the pinnacle of his career with a Giro-World Championship road race double. This victory in the Giro d'Italia was his last, bringing his total wins in the race to five.

From 1954 onwards, his dominance in Italian cycling began to wane slowly. After all, Fausto was now over 35 years old. Victories in major races gradually dwindled. The younger generation was knocking at the door, and serious injuries started to accumulate. Falls and withdrawals became more frequent. Off-the-bike issues also overshadowed his performances, notably his affair with Giulia Occhini, the "White Lady." This romance did not sit well with a puritanical, conformist, Christian Democratic Italy. After being adored like a deity, Fausto Coppi found himself isolated from his public's affection.

In December 1959, he replaced Louison Bobet at the last minute in a criterium organized by Raphaël Géminiani in Upper Volta (now Burkina Faso). Upon returning home, he suddenly began to shake on the afternoon of December 25, 1959.

Although the circumstances and symptoms pointed towards a diagnosis of malaria, the surgeon treating him stubbornly administered another treatment, injecting massive doses of cortisone. Due to the ineffectiveness of the treatment, Fausto Coppi passed away on January 2, 1960, at the hospital in Tortona. He was only 40 years old.

After his death, the nickname Campionissimo, bestowed upon him by journalists, was never used for any other rider.

In 2002, Fausto was among the riders inducted into the Union Cycliste Internationale's Hall of Fame.

Among other tributes, and to celebrate the 100th anniversary of his birth, his birthplace of Castellania was renamed Castellania Coppi in 2019. Reflecting an unparalleled career, Fausto is one of the few, if not the only, athletes in the world to have a locality named after him.

2

High-Powered German Machine: Jan Ullrich

In 1997, a German rider, just 22 years old, took the cycling world by storm.

Jan Ullrich had just won the Tour de France, with a margin over the runner-up not seen in a long time. His dominance was such that even Bernard Hinault remarked, "This beardless red-head has the potential to win ten Tours de France."

Ullrich clinched this title with panache. During the 10th stage, finishing in Andorra, he not only grabbed the yellow jersey but also set a record: the most powerful climb in the history of cycling. Nearly superhuman. This display of power was again evident two days later, during an epic time trial...

Jan Ullrich was born in Rostock, in former East Germany. In 1993, he became the amateur world champion in Oslo, after a sprint that showcased his main attribute: incredible, completely unbridled power.

He turned professional the following year and finished 3rd in the world time trial championships. Then, precociously, in 1996, he revealed his full potential at one of the year's main events: the Tour de France.

In that edition, won by his teammate Riis, Ullrich was the linchpin of the victory for "Mr. 60%". Besides, he had some personal highlights. While prioritizing his role as a teammate, he took part in some successful breaks and managed to hold off Miguel Indurain, the five-time defending champion.

At just 21 years old, and on his first Tour appearance, Ullrich achieved his first podium finish with a second place. Thus, the 1996 edition was excellent for the German Telekom team, placing two riders in the top two spots.

The narrow gap between the two teammates – just 1'40" – raised questions. Could this young, unknown rider with the lion's mane have won the race if he hadn't loyally worked for Riis?

The answer came the following year. Telekom presented Jan as a co-leader. The team's management didn't show favoritism, counting on a good understanding between the young German and the Danish champion.

Bjarne Riis was, of course, a reliable value. He had impressed greatly by winning the last Amstel Gold Race solo. But it was clear that Ullrich deserved his chances. The Telekom team knew they had found a real gem. A raw gem. Raw with power. Possibly one of the best cyclists in the world in the making.

In the early stages, the Danish titleholder lost time to Ullrich, notably due to a puncture. Some tension arose, but sports director Walter Godefroot continued to defend the co-leadership project.

In the first Pyrenean stage, the real contenders came to the forefront. The Telekom leaders would clearly have their work cut out with the Festina team of Richard Virenque. Besides these two teams, some individuals emerged, like Marco Pantani or Fernando Escartín.

Stage 9 went from Pau to Loudenvielle via, in order, the Soulor, Tourmalet, Aspin, and Val-Louron-Azet cols. That day, Ullrich was asked to play the role of a "water carrier" to aid Riis, who was showing serious signs of weakness.

The young German complied, simply following orders, though he seemed capable of accelerating and making a difference at any moment. Each time he took the lead in the peloton, a gap formed soon after. However, he had to slow down several times because Riis couldn't keep up with his pace—a harbinger of an impending leadership transfer...

About seven kilometers from the summit of Val-Louron-Azet, Laurent Brochard from Festina took off alone. A group of three top riders quickly formed to chase him down: Virenque, Pantani, and... Ullrich. In the heat of the moment, Ullrich left his teammate behind to try his luck.

The pursuers caught up with Brochard just before the summit and rode a few kilometers together. In this breakaway, there was a lot of looking and measuring up. Suddenly, three kilometers from the finish, the Frenchman attacked again. He got on his thighs and took off!

...que covered him, Pantani didn't react. As for Jan Ullrich, he had to ...his tongue. His sports director had asked him to hang back and ...eserve the status quo. Although he meticulously followed the directives and played as a team for this time, his moment of personal glory was approaching.

Stage 10 started in Luchon and ended in Andorra. 252 km, with difficulties, but a manageable layout overall.

A wind of change was blowing within Telekom. Jan was quickly gaining the upper hand over Bjarne. The young rider's ego was flattered. Moreover, thanks to his hard work, the yellow jersey was now just 13 seconds away. After closing the gap on Cédric Vasseur, Jan was about to deliver the final blow today.

The two co-leaders of Deutsche Telekom rode together at the beginning of the stage. They were seen discussing and exchanging at length. One might think they were devising a strategy for today. But Riis, like all riders in the bunch, didn't have enough juice to follow Ullrich. And he knew it. So maybe he was simply willing to let his protégé spread his wings. After all, he had done so much for him in the previous Tour...

As often happens, the race situation clarifies in the last kilometers. In the climb to Ordino, the Frenchman Jean-Philippe Dojwa breaks away alone. He is followed, at kilometer 240, by the yellow jersey himself. Vasseur knows his 13-second lead doesn't weigh much in the balance. But if he must relinquish his seat, it will be with dignity, weapons in hand.

Behind, Jan Ullrich takes turns leading a group of about twenty pursuers. This group consists of the cream of the climbers. Everyone clings on, trying to keep up with the pace set by the German. Ullrich, hammering, taking aggressive turns, is literally tearing the peloton apart.

Jan is undoubtedly in the form of his life. He feels it in his legs. He doesn't want to attack to not put Riis in difficulty, but he can't help himself. He informs Godefroot that he's going to attack.

Shortly after passing the ten-kilometer banner, coming out of a turn, he briefly stands up and accelerates hard. He distances his group by a few meters, then repeats the maneuver coming out of the next turn. Only Virenque manages to follow him, a few meters behind. But when Ullrich sits down and shows his power, the Frenchman from Festina can do nothing.

Ullrich overtakes Vasseur. He is now alone. In the curves of the Andorra climb, he is a true beast.

Behind, Richard Virenque tries to restart with Pantani and Fincato. The latter quickly falls behind. The other two exchange a few words. These temporary allies organize relays to try to catch up with Jan. It's to no avail. The gap continues to widen.

Dojwa is now within shooting range. Ullrich overtakes him without even a glance. Jean-Philippe is stunned. "I saw Ullrich pass by pedaling three times faster than me," he said after the race.

No matter that he's been on his bike for almost eight hours. He continues to push the pedals and takes the turns on the inside. The gap with his two pursuers, now competing for a runner-up spot in the general classification, is growing visibly, and they can do nothing about it.

Having failed to catch the escapee, Pantani crosses the line in second place, with Virenque on his wheel, both 1'07" behind. In the general classification, Ullrich, after his demonstration, takes the yellow jersey. In 1997, a young German cyclist, just 22 years old, surprised the world of cycling.

Jan Ullrich had just won the Tour de France, with a margin over the runner-up, Richard Virenque, of 2'58", and the third-placed, Spanish Abraham Olano, at 4'46". Ullrich's solo finish, with the national champion's jersey on his shoulders and arms stretched to the sky, sparked unprecedented enthusiasm for cycling in Germany.

His performance was staggering, achieving the most powerful climb ever recorded in cycling history, with an average power output of 445 watts. This power, combined with his signature posture—seated on the saddle, hands on the bottom of the handlebars, in a high gear, pedaling with pure force—highlighted his extraordinary natural strength in the loins and hips.

The French press bowed to this feat, yet questions lingered about the young German's limits and his ability to maintain the pace all the way to Paris. These were answered emphatically two days later during the 12th stage, a 55-kilometer individual time trial in Saint-Etienne.

Wearing the "maillot jaune", Ullrich started last, as is customary. Virenque, second in the general classification, had started three minutes earlier. Ullrich's overwhelming power was on full display, and about eleven kilometers from the finish, he overtook Virenque, the polka dot jersey wearer, maintaining a respectful distance to the finish line.

Ullrich's sensational performance extended his lead by 3'04" over Virenque, who paradoxically achieved his best time trial performance, placing second in the stage. This victory further widened Ullrich's lead in the general classification, with Virenque 5'42" behind and Olano at 8 minutes.

The battle in the Alps, seemingly pre-determined for the Telekom rider, involved Festina working for Virenque, Ullrich supported by his teammates including Riis, and Marco Pantani as a lone wolf. Despite these challenges, Ullrich's dominance remained unchallenged.

Pantani won the 13th stage to Alpe d'Huez, setting a new record. The next day, Festina started strong, but Telekom quickly organized. In Courchevel, Ullrich and Virenque dueled, with the latter winning the stage. The 15th stage saw Pantani win again, moving into third overall, with Ullrich and Virenque forming a chasing duo. Despite Virenque's attempts, Ullrich countered every attack.

As the Tour headed north through the Vosges and Switzerland, Festina animated the stages, hoping to upset the standings, but Ullrich's lead remained secure.

On the eve of the final stage, Ullrich led Virenque by 9'09", a margin that held to Paris, with Pantani finishing third overall at 14'03". Ullrich's victory marked him as the youngest Tour winner since Laurent Fignon and the first German to achieve this feat.

However, the bright future anticipated for Ullrich dimmed quickly. The following year, without Virenque (embroiled in the Festina scandal), Ullrich appeared out of shape and finished second to a resurgent Pantani. Injuries, insufficient preparation, and the dominance of Lance Armstrong relegated Ullrich to the runner-up position in 2000, 2001, and 2003, and fourth in 2004. He returned to the podium in 2005 in third place, but was later disqualified.

Despite setbacks in the Tour de France, Ullrich found success elsewhere, winning the Vuelta in 1999 and becoming world time trial champion in 1999 and 2001. He also won Olympic gold and silver medals in Sydney 2000 and claimed the Tour de Suisse in 2004.

Aiming for a second Tour de France win after Armstrong's retirement, Ullrich's preparations were cut short by his involvement in the Operación Puerto scandal, leading to his dismissal from T-Mobile and exclusion from the Tour.

After failed negotiations with Discovery Channel and other teams, Ullrich retired in February 2007, leaving a legacy of what might have been. His career, marked by unfulfilled potential and controversy, remains a topic of speculation and a poignant chapter in cycling history.

3

The Cannibal and The Old Lady: Eddy Merckx

The scene unfolds in Sallanches, Haute-Savoie, on September 5, 1964. A young Belgian cyclist, just 19 years old, crosses the finish line of the amateur world championship alone. His closest competitors would arrive 27 seconds later.

The new world champion had established his lead solo, having shaken off all his rivals on the climb of Passy. Journalist Léon Zitrone, commentating on the event, was astonished and predicted a bright future for him: "Eddy Merckx, remember this name well!"

Zitrone could hardly imagine the impact this name would have on the cycling legend. He did not foresee that the Belgian's fame would extend beyond the realm of the "little queen." Léon had just encountered someone who would become one of the most famous cyclists of all time. And, decades later, his name is still perfectly remembered.

No superlative has been spared in describing him. He is the cyclist with the most professional victories; the champion among champions. The

Belgian set a high bar, with only a few great riders displaying a similar record. Among them, only one could contest his title as "the greatest cyclist of all time": Fausto Coppi.

The topic gently divides the hardcore cycling community. While the Italian is deemed more impressive in effort, Merckx is superior in terms of achievements.

When discussing numbers, it's essential to be good at counting when looking at his career, as the Belgian amassed a vast palmarès. In just thirteen seasons of professional cycling, focusing only on the major titles, he won the Super Prestige Pernod, the point-based world championship of the time, for seven consecutive years from 1969 to 1975.

His list of major victories continues with three World Road Race Championships (in 1967, 1971, and 1974). Equally adept on the road as on the track, he dominated the World Madison Championship twice, in 1969 and 1977, and the Omnium in 1975.

It was also on the velodrome slopes where Edouard, alias Eddy, achieved one of his greatest performances. On October 25, 1972, within the Agustín Melgar Velodrome in Mexico, he broke the hour record.

His exceptional resistance to the pain of effort allowed him to push his physiological limits that day. Exhausted, with a terribly sore back and unable to stand, he gave the first post-record interviews lying on the track.

Merckx covered a distance of 49.431 km in 60 minutes, surpassing the previous record-holder, Danish Ole Ritter, who had covered 48.653 kilometers under the same conditions, by nearly 800 meters.

The difference was substantial, thanks in part to Merckx's exceptional physical capabilities and a preparation that bordered on torture. At his home in Crainhem, he even trained with a mask simulating the atmospheric conditions and oxygen scarcity of Mexico's altitude.

On the technical side, one of the most skilled mechanics of all time, Ernesto Colnago, contributed to the triumph in Mexico. He crafted a bike for Merckx that weighed merely 5.8 kg. This bike, reputed to be the most expensive in the world at the time, is now displayed at the Eddy Merckx metro station in Brussels.

Although this hour record would be surpassed in the 1990s by Chris Boardman and Graeme Obree, UCI's revision of the official record-keeping criteria left Merckx as the record holder until 2000.

He also boasts another, unofficial distinction: the Triple Crown. In 1974, he became the first to win a World Championship and two Grand Tours in the same season—a feat only matched by Stephen Roche in 1987. Yet, Merckx remains the only cyclist to have achieved the Giro-Tour double in the same year three times, surpassing Coppi, Hinault, and Indurain, who achieved it "only" twice.

In terms of Grand Tour victories, who else but Eddy Merckx tops the list? With five Tour de France wins (1969, 1970, 1971, 1972, 1974), five Giro victories (1968, 1970, 1972, 1973, 1974), and one Vuelta (1973), he seems unbeatable as the record holder.

His successes, like so many stones added to the edifice of his legend, were brilliantly won. Sparkling in time trials, flamboyant in the mountains, and speedy in sprints, he didn't just manage his races; he won a total of sixty-four Grand Tour stages over his career.

Adding to his one-day race successes, his career statistics are staggering: 625 race wins—525 on the road, 98 on the track, and 2 in cyclo-cross, counting both his amateur and professional careers. In his professional years, he won 28% of the races he entered, nearly one in every three. This insatiable quest for glory earned him the nickname "The Cannibal" from French cyclist Christian Raymond, a fitting moniker that stuck.

Merckx's unparalleled ability to sustain intense efforts over long distances left all his competitors in the dust. His resistance to pain made him an extraordinary classics rider, where most races exceed 200 km and offer no second chances. He punctually won a total of 27 classics, including Milan-San Remo seven times—a record still standing. He also shares the record for the most victories in Ghent-Wevelgem (three times, in 1967, 1970, and 1973) and demonstrated his selfish domination in Liège-Bastogne-Liège.

This race is one of the five "Monument" classics, the most prestigious races on the cycling calendar. Highly coveted, these events are renowned for their daunting reputation. Exhausting by nature, a Monument classic is invariably settled through sweat and suffering, and sometimes tears and blood.

Liège-Bastogne-Liège, one of the oldest classics in the professional circuit, was created in 1892 and rightly nicknamed "La Doyenne" (The Old Lady). Its route, approximately 250 km long, is demanding and punishing. Starting from Liège, cyclists head south before turning back at Bastogne. From there, they must return to the "Fiery City," facing the steep hills of the Ardennes—a true death march.

Among the iconic grunts, the peloton encounters the notorious Côte de la Redoute, famous for its average gradient of 8.8% over about 2 km. This is only an average, as some sections approach a 20% gradient. Only the best punchers can conquer it without being left breathless.

The Côte de Saint Nicolas is also worth mentioning. This steep, brutal climb, located just a few kilometers from the finish, often proves decisive for the final victory. After navigating narrow, winding roads, exhausting climbs, and typically unpredictable, sometimes hellish weather, the Côte de Saint Nicolas is a critical test for those still in contention.

Indeed, only a few brave souls, possessing sufficient physical resilience and mental endurance, manage to complete the race. La Doyenne does not easily reveal its secrets. Only the best climbers and punchers in the peloton can withstand the relentless attacks while making their move on the steepest sections. Typically, only between half to a third of the riders manage to reach Liège to contest the finish. In the most grueling years, even fewer make it to the end.

Eddy Merckx participated in his first Liège-Bastogne-Liège in 1966, finishing in eighth place—a commendable result, as he was among the 28 competitors who reached the finish line out of 87 starters.

The following year, Merckx's career skyrocketed. Early in the season, he won Milan-San Remo, Ghent-Wevelgem, and the Flèche Wallonne but narrowly missed victory at La Doyenne. Due to adverse weather conditions, the finish at the Rocourt velodrome was slightly altered. Merckx, learning of this last minute, was momentarily thrown off, allowing Godefroot to sprint past him and win.

Merckx did not participate in the classic in 1968. He returned in 1969, this time determined to win. At 23, he was in peak form, as evidenced by another explosive start to the season. With the vigor of youth, he had already shaken up the hierarchy and amassed a wealth of success. Through victories and defeats, he had built up solid experience and unshakeable mental strength. A victory at Liège-Bastogne-Liège was one of his main goals. "I'm going to show them who Eddy Merckx really is," he declared on the eve of the race. The message was clear.

Racing for the Faema team since the previous year, he had a top-tier support squad, ready to go to great lengths for him. And on April 22, 1969, the Belgian team delivered an impressive performance.

In the early part of the race, a breakaway of five riders formed, including Victor Van Schil and Roger Swerts from Faema. Merckx, remaining behind, showed patience. Utilizing the climbs of Wanne and Stockeu, he shed his main rivals and joined the breakaway group, which he soon shattered.

With 100 km remaining, the Cannibal found himself in the lead, flanked only by Van Schil and Swerts. Swerts, having worked tirelessly, encountered derailleur issues and quickly fell back, leaving his two teammates to power ahead. By the top of the Côte de la Grande Levée, the duo had already established a one-minute lead, which would only grow by Liège.

As it became apparent that this bold escape would succeed, speculation arose about whether the sprint would be contested between the two. Merckx, in a show of sportsmanship, wanted to let Van Schil cross the line first. However, Victor firmly insisted, "Of course, you're going to win, and if you fall and break your leg, I'll carry you to the finish line." At Faema, the hierarchy was clear, and the team united. The domestiques worked hard, occasionally taking honors, while the leader claimed the victories.

In the Rocourt velodrome, the two men made their final lap like a victory lap, enjoying the moment. Merckx led Victor, and they raised their hands together at the finish line.

The gap was so significant that Merckx had time to remove his gear and join the journalists, commentating on the arrival of the third-place rider, Barry Hoban, who finished 8'05" behind.

In 1970, the Cannibal was eager to claim La Doyenne for the second time, but this edition would be marked by a controversial sporting incident.

The story begins the previous year when Belgian Roger de Vlaeminck refused to join Faema, knowing Merckx was the undisputed leader and unwilling to play second fiddle.

De Vlaeminck's results justified his decision, including winning the 1969 Belgian National Road Race Championship. His popularity quickly soared, challenging Merckx's status among Belgian fans.

When the two rivals lined up for the 1970 Liège-Bastogne-Liège, de Vlaeminck had just been humiliated at Paris-Roubaix. Days earlier, Merckx had dominated the Hell of the North, winning with a 5'21" margin over the second-placed de Vlaeminck. Wounded in pride, the Belgian champion was determined to redeem himself, even at the expense of sportsmanship.

Approaching the finish, the race situation had cleared. Victory would be contested among six riders, all Belgians, who had significantly distanced the remnants of the peloton: Frans Verbeeck (Geens-Watneys-Diamant), Georges Pintens, Herman Van Springel (both from Mann-Grundig), Roger and Eric de Vlaeminck (Flandria-Mars), and, of course, Eddy Merckx (Faema-Faemino).

To enter the Liège velodrome, riders had to pass through a tunnel beneath the stadium stands. During this brief "blind" passage, where onboard cameras couldn't film and the stadium's fixed cameras hadn't yet taken over, Roger de Vlaeminck launched an attack. Merckx responded, but Eric de Vlaeminck was quicker. Seeing his brother break away, Eric "blocked" Merckx in a clear, yet unpunished obstruction, preventing him from following Roger de Vlaeminck, who went on to win, leaving Merckx 12 seconds behind due to the delay in the tunnel.

Merckx seldom discussed the incident, even decades later, adhering to a sportsmanlike spirit and settling the dispute on the road. He did just that two days later by winning the Flèche Wallonne solo.

The rivalry between Roger de Vlaeminck and Eddy Merckx, fueled by statements from one and frustration from the other, was relentless. The tunnel incident at Rocourt remained a sore point for Merckx, who entered the 1971 edition of La Doyenne determined and aggressive. However, in a moment of overconfidence, possibly overestimating his strength, he nearly faltered.

The Cannibal decided to apply the same strategy that earned him victory in 1969. On the Côte de Stockeu, he dropped everyone and went solo. With nearly 92 km left to battle alone against the elements, the weather was atrocious. For an April day, it was bitterly cold, and the falling rain turned to snow.

As usual, Eddy quickly put a significant distance between himself and the peloton, at one point leading by as much as 4'35". However, this advantage would gradually diminish. Uncharacteristically, Merckx experienced a major dip in performance. Struggling on the climb of Mont Theux, he learned that a pursuer, Georges Pintens (from Hertekamp-Magniflex), was hot on his trail.

With his lead reduced to just a minute, he wisely decided to ease off. He allowed Pintens to catch up, knowing he couldn't make it to the end alone.

The catch was made five kilometers from the finish. Georges Pintens was a strong rider, recently hitting a peak form. He gave Merckx a much-needed boost, allowing him to recover. Merckx stayed behind his compatriot, getting a perfect lead-out onto the Rocourt track.

The Hertekamp-Magniflex rider, giving it his all, was buoyed by the hope of winning Liège-Bastogne-Liège. With just one track lap away from triumph, alas, he was up against the world's best cyclist. Even diminished, Merckx remained a sprint specialist. Coming out of a turn, he surged past Pintens with a powerful acceleration. The attack was decisive, and he won by a good length against Georges Pintens.

Though the sprint was won easily, the Cannibal was aware that his race management was less than perfect. While he usually appeared to be far above the rest, this time, he suffered like never before to secure the victory. This Liège-Bastogne-Liège proved to be one of the toughest wins of his career.

Eddy Merckx had a particular fondness for the Côte de Stockeu. While the gradient slowed the peloton and weakened his competitors, he would overpower everyone with explosive attacks known only to him. It was his favorite launchpad, so much so that a monument in his honor now stands there.

In 1972, on this favored terrain, Merckx decided to make his move on the same climb, a narrow country road flanked by pastures. As his competitors struggled, the Brussels native stood on his pedals and accelerated. That year, no one could follow. Wearing the rainbow jersey of the world champion, Eddy was determined to honor it.

However, his solo breakaway was no easy feat. A recent fall at Paris-Nice had left its mark. Despite lighter training, his injuries frequently flared up, hindering him.

When the Cannibal broke away from the group, he knew he'd have to rely on his extraordinary pain tolerance. After climbing Stockeu, he struggled to create a significant gap from the bunch. The world champion suffered but held on. It was only after crossing the Côte d'Annette and Lubin in Spa that he sealed his triumph. The lead he had painstakingly built was comfortable enough for a final victory in... Verviers.

Indeed, the 1972 Liège-Bastogne-Liège finish was exceptionally moved to Verviers, located 25 kilometers east of the "Fiery City."

This change was specifically requested and supported by Jean Crahay, a close friend of Merckx. This cycling race organizer wanted to highlight his town and attract more significant races. Despite fan protests, the Doyenne's finish would return to Liège the following year. However,

Crahay's gamble paid off, as Verviers hosted the start of the 1973 Giro, much to Merckx's delight.

The enthusiastic people of Verviers warmly welcomed the Cannibal's solo arrival. The day had been tough for him, but his daring once again proved decisive. After the finish, he enjoyed the moment, greeting the crowd gathered in small stands and taking time to engage extensively with the spectators.

The race's outcome was long in coming, but the champion still won by a large margin. The runner-up, Wim Schepers, finished 2'40" behind. Eddy Merckx added his third Liège-Bastogne-Liège victory to his trophy gallery, including two consecutive wins.

The popular saying goes, "there's never two without three." But could the Cannibal win this classic three times in a row?

The launch of the 1973 season was similar to the previous year. Sick, Eddy had to withdraw from Milan-San Remo. Then, barely recovered, he settled for third place in the Tour of Flanders. What followed? Back in top form, he had a voracious appetite, achieving his best season in the classics, nearly sweeping them all.

This edition of La Doyenne began boldly. From the fifth kilometer, a group of five, then six riders, broke away. The peloton let them gain air, amassing a 6'15" lead before being reeled in at kilometer 95.

Aside from this breakaway, the race was uneventful. Everyone eagerly anticipated the climb of Côte de Stockeu, a key moment expected to spark action. The riders knew it too, better than anyone. They also knew this steep incline, a leg-cutter, was Eddy Merckx's favorite spot for his formidable "follow me if you can" challenges.

Once again, the Cannibal didn't hesitate to use his favorite climb. But this time, his attack was anticipated. Everyone was waiting for him. And his toughest opponents managed to stick with him.

Thanks to effective groundwork and a more pronounced acceleration, he managed to make a tighter selection and a clearer break in the Côte de la Haute Levée. Merckx took the lead, joined by Ocaña, Poulidor, and Zoetemelk. Sweating profusely, they established a 1'25" lead over a "peloton" of about twenty riders.

Led by a handful of underdogs, this group caught up with the escapees near Theux. The newly formed group quickly disintegrated, leaving the elite of cycling to form a tight lead group. In the climb of Côte des Forges, the last challenge before the finish, the situation remained unchanged.

This time, Merckx's plan didn't work. To match Léon Houa's three consecutive victories in La Doyenne, he had to snatch the final victory in a sprint.

The 1973 Liège-Bastogne-Liège finish, for the last time at the Rocourt velodrome, saw the best contenders duke it out on its track.

Poulidor, Ocaña, Zoetemelk, and Bernard Thévenet were all present, with other competitors staying discreet yet dangerous. They were formidable finishers, ready to seize any opportunity: Mortensen, Houbrechts, Van Schil, Ovion Verbeeck, Pintens, Van Springel, and Godefroot, the 1967 winner here.

Verbeeck entered the track first and quickly moved aside, unwilling to lead out the rest. As Merckx overtook Verbeeck, a slowdown occurred. Merckx, who was second, found himself in front. It was the least favorable position for a sprint; he felt like prey pursued by twelve hardened hunters.

To maintain hope of victory against this hungry pack, Eddy had to surprise them. He had to avoid being swallowed by the group while knowing that keeping his position would serve his adversaries. They would just need to stay in his slipstream and launch a fatal acceleration at the right moment.

Since the Cannibal was leading, he had to keep it until the end. He had to push the boundaries of suffering once again. To maintain his position, he began to increase his pedaling intensity. But was it too early? Was it madness? No one was truly optimistic about his chances of crossing the line first...

In his wake, the followers organized and positioned themselves. Verbeeck, Thévenet, and Mortensen were directly behind him. Godefroot made an unsuccessful attempt, trying to "climb the balustrades." Eddy managed to contain everyone for the moment. But he knew it would be very difficult to do until the finish.

His pursuers were fast and punchy over short distances. To neutralize them, he had to wear them out well before they could initiate the sprint. It was his only chance.

To create some space and relieve the pressure, the Cannibal stood up on his pedals. He increased his cadence again, even though the line was still far away. But Verbeeck stuck close. He couldn't shake him off.

The outcome was decided coming out of the last turn. Merckx tensed, hunched over his handlebars, and pushed his pedals furiously. Verbeeck, who had positioned himself well for the sprint, attacked as expected. He moved outside. The bikes, swaying under the power exerted by the riders, brushed against each other. First the front wheels, then the handlebars. Finally, in a last-ditch effort, Eddy and Frans "threw" their bikes. Each, in a desperate move, gave one last push on their handlebars. The few millimeters gained would turn out to be the most important of their careers.

At first glance, the judges declared it impossible to determine the winner. The gap was so tiny that a decision based on naked-eye observations was impossible. They resorted to the photo finish.

The minutes of deliberation were endless. Half of the stands had descended onto the track and crowded around the riders. The wait was unbearable, especially since the final was so close.

When the winner's name was finally announced, the crowd was almost surprised. Verbeeck was coming back so strong on Merckx, he seemed so powerful, that it seemed he had overtaken him at the line. But the Cannibal was an exceptional all-rounder...

At the cost of an effort unbearable for mere mortals, he managed to keep all his rivals at bay until the end. And at the line, he managed to edge out Frans Verbeeck. Indeed, Eddy's wheel was just a few centimeters ahead of Frans's. For the fourth time, including three in a row, he won La Doyenne.

Serious lung problems prevented the champion from potentially winning a fourth consecutive title in the Liège race. Forced to rest, the Cannibal couldn't defend his title in 1974. But he quickly returned, arriving at La Doyenne in peak form in 1975, after a spring full of victories.

The peloton encountered an unprecedented challenge: the Côte de la Redoute. This merciless grunt stretches for 1.7 km, with an average gradient of 9% but includes stretches as steep as 22%! This section has become a crucial juncture in the race.

In this iteration, Merckx didn't employ his signature move on the Côte de Stockeu. Though years have passed, and he undoubtedly remains the leader of the pack, capable of shaking off his most formidable rivals, the margins by which he outpaces them have diminished from days past.

The finish line is now situated on Boulevard de la Sauvenière in Liège. With no riders managing to break away solo, a tightly-knit group of eleven cyclists makes its way into the final kilometers. Among them is Bernard Thévenet, alongside several climbers who have kept pace with the Cannibal. Sprinters have also made their presence known, speedy competitors looking to seize their moment in the final sprint, including the stalwarts of Belgian cycling: Frans Verbeeck, Roger de Vlaeminck, and Walter Godefroot.

Signifying a change in the tides, Merckx attempts to pull away from this group three times. Each effort is thwarted, and he's reeled back in every time. The race's climax becomes one of the most electrifying finales in the annals of La Doyenne, showcasing a tit-for-tat battle among these top-tier competitors.

Eddy's fourth effort finally cracks the group wide open. Deciding against vying for victory against seasoned sprinters proves too perilous.

When he makes his move, only Bernard Thévenet, no stranger to competition, can follow his wheel. The Frenchman even manages to outmaneuver Eddy momentarily. But Merckx isn't ready to hand over the reins just yet.

He catches up with Thévenet in time to jockey for position in the sprint. The Cannibal, ever the indomitable lion, unfazed and almost serene, yet capable of explosive speed, devours Thévenet in the sprint, crossing the finish line with ease.

That's five victories! A titanic force at the zenith of his career, Merckx clinches this "Monument" classic for the fifth time—a feat unmatched by any other. No one has conquered this notoriously demanding course five times. After this fifth triumph, the Belgian's record in this race is nothing short of audacious: 5 victories in 7 attempts.

The following year marks the beginning of a downturn in his storied career. He places eighth in Liège-Bastogne-Liège—his poorest showing—followed by two sixth-place finishes in subsequent years. As Merckx himself reflects, "Victories are becoming less frequent, failures more routine." Slowly, he must yield to the emerging talents, yet his legendary exploits remain set in stone, resonating even today for some.

Eddy Merckx is synonymous with unparalleled achievement. His legacy can be succinctly summed up by the races he hasn't won. A dominator of his era's Grand Tours, insatiable in his pursuit of victories at Milan-San Remo, he is indubitably the man of Liège-Bastogne-Liège. The definitive man of La Doyenne.

4

Time Trials and Records: Chris Boardman

The 1994 Tour de France took off with a spectacle on July 2nd, turning heads right from its traditional prologue in Lille, spanning a brisk 7.2 km. While all eyes were on favorites like Indurain, Zülle, and Rominger, it was a Brit, Chris Boardman, who ended up grabbing the headlines.

Boardman, relatively unknown in the Tour scene, blew the competition away with a stunning display of strength and skill. The prologue's challenging layout, characterized by tight turns and cobblestone patches, didn't seem to phase him. Racing through the course in 7'49", he clocked an average speed of 55.152 km/h, obliterating the previous record of 52.365 km/h set by Frenchman Thierry Marie back in 1991.

Astride the now-iconic Lotus bike, tipping the scales at just over 9 kg, Boardman's sleek aerodynamics and smooth pedal strokes were a sight to behold on the urban circuit. Impressively, he even managed to overtake Luc Leblanc, known for his climbing prowess, who had started before him, just before crossing the finish line.

Pushing giants like Indurain 15 seconds back and Rominger 19 seconds behind, Boardman clinched the yellow jersey, marking the first time a Brit had done so since Tim Simpson in 1962.

This prologue triumph wasn't just another win; it was a sensation. Celebrated by the media, especially back in Britain, the quiet hero became an overnight sensation. For many, Chris Boardman, who had turned pro only in 1993 with Team Gan, seemed to have come out of nowhere.

Thrust into the spotlight, Boardman was determined not to fade into the backdrop of the peloton. With the toughest stages still ahead, he aimed to fight tooth and nail to keep his sunny jersey for as long as he could: "I'm ecstatic about the win, but the Tour de France is a long and arduous journey. This is merely the start, and I've got to battle to stay out front."

And battle he did. Boardman held his lead until the team time trial on the 3rd stage, which stretched 66.5 km from Calais to the Channel Tunnel. With the fourth and fifth stages set on his home turf in England, he was eager to wear the yellow in front of his home crowd.

Boardman went into the time trial with gusto. However, his relentless pace proved too much for some of his teammates. With a few dropping back and exchanges becoming erratic, the team's performance fell short. Ranking eighth, Chris had to hand over his leader's jersey.

Team Gan saw its leader, Greg LeMond, drop out during the sixth stage, and not long after, the prologue's record-setter, now known as "The Professor," also bowed out before stage 11's conclusion.

Yet, Boardman's Tour tale was far from over. He returned the following year with a top-ten finish in his sights, declaring, "Perhaps not first, but at least among the top ten." In England, fans disregarded this modesty, hoping to see him clinch the race.

Alas, the 1995 prologue's initial kilometers saw him pushing the limits, hitting speeds near 80 km/h, only to take a "gravity check" due to unexpected rain, resulting in a double ankle fracture.

By 1996, Boardman completed his first Tour, albeit in a modest 39th place. The next year, he triumphed in the prologue again in Rouen, donning the yellow for a day before Marco Cipollini overtook him, leading to another withdrawal by stage 13.

1998 echoed previous years' narratives. In Dublin, Boardman snagged yet another prologue win. His mastery of the discipline was unmatched by his contemporaries. He maintained his lead after the first stage, only to suffer a severe crash en route to Cork the next day, forcing another withdrawal.

Finally, in 1999, he once again crossed the Tour's finish line, albeit in a less than stellar 119th place. The result was a letdown, but "The Professor" kept it in perspective, acknowledging his hormonal profile didn't favor endurance: "It's been this way since birth, but it wasn't a problem for the type of races I previously competed in."

Boardman's forte was undoubtedly the individual battle against the clock. While he had his moments in stage races, his greatest achievements were in time trials, both on the road and the velodrome track.

***

Born in Hoylake in 1968, Chris Boardman shone from an early age. In 1984, he snagged his first national title in the time trial at the 10-mile cadet championships. By 1986, he was the British champion over 25 miles in the junior category.

Moving into the senior category in 1988, he confirmed all the potential he had shown so far. Between 1988 and 1991, he clinched four consecutive national hill climb titles. Alongside, he also secured five straight British championships over 25 miles (from 1989 to 1993), as well as winning the 50-mile championship twice, in 1991 and 1992.

His dominance in individual time trials shouldn't overshadow his achievements in team events. With the Manchester Wheelers' Club, he triumphed three times in the 100 km team time trial event, in 1988, 1989, and 1991. In 1993, he did it again with another club, North Wirral Velo. In this last edition, his team set a record for the event, clocking in at 2 hours and 7 minutes.

Boardman also clinched an international title in 1990, bringing home a bronze medal from the Commonwealth Games in the team time trial.

His major breakthrough came at the 1992 Barcelona Olympics. Still an amateur rider, he managed to catch up with German Jens Lehmann in the final of the individual pursuit. At the open-air velodrome in Horta, he ascended to the rank of Olympic champion in the discipline.

While striving for Olympic glory, the British cyclist dreamt big, aiming for the professional ranks. Unfortunately, British cyclists weren't highly visible at the time, and few managed to sign with professional teams.

The most common path to turning pro involved moving to France, winning as many amateur races as possible to get noticed.

However, this option meant facing loneliness, far from loved ones, in challenging living conditions. Boardman, not keen on isolation and already a family man, chose another path. He decided to excel in time trials, to be among the best, to make a name for himself. In essence, to be his best representative.

This boldness, coupled with intense training, paid off. The Gan team, led by Roger Legeay, signed him for the 1993 season. Expected to excel in time trials, he met his team's expectations right away.

He raced his first professional event that same year, the Grand Prix Eddy Merckx, a 66 km time trial. Despite being a newbie on the pro circuit, he won the race!

His career took a new turn. His horizon broadened. This new status opened doors to world championships and allowed him to compete in numerous high-profile races. He won several, including the Criterium International, the Grand Prix Eddy Merckx, and the Grand Prix des Nations in 1996. Besides, Boardman notched an array of second-place finishes at the Criterium du Dauphiné in 1995, the Tour de Romandie and the Grand Prix Eddy Merckx in 1997, and the Grand Prix des Nations in 1999.

These impressive results in stage races were hard-won. When faced with long days in the saddle, Boardman had to dig deep. But when it came to battling against the clock, especially solo, he was in his element.

Chris racked up an incredible number of time trial victories across all his races. Competing—and beating—the best, he broke records, amassed titles, and collected medals.

Less than two months after his notable victory in the 1994 Tour prologue, he was crowned world champion in Agrigento, Italy, in the individual time trial, naturally! He went on to win silver in the same event in 1996 and bronze in 1997 and 1999.

He also clinched a bronze at the Atlanta Olympics in road cycling. For the 1996 Games, Chris decided not to defend his pursuit title, focusing instead on the 52 km road event.

The Hoylake native loved challenging the clock on the road, but his favorite arena remained the steeped tracks of velodromes, where he achieved his greatest successes, earning him the nickname "The Professor."

This affectionate moniker came partly from his meticulous physical preparation and significant innovations, even inventions, he introduced to his bikes. For instance, during the victorious 1994 prologue, his bike featured a handlebar of his design, minimalist brake levers, and an electric gear shifting system.

Earlier, in 1992, he brought to Barcelona a bike that caused a sensation: the Lotus Type 108. Lotus, as in the Formula 1 car manufacturer, collaborated in a sort of British holy alliance to develop an innovative bike.

Since 1990, the UCI had permitted monocoque frames. Engineers resurrected a dormant project, pushing their research to the limit, culminating in the Type 108.

The prototype was a marvel of innovation, boasting a revolutionary silhouette with an ultra-light carbon fiber frame, carbon wheels, a triathlon handlebar, a single-blade fork, and a single rear stay on the drivetrain side. This resulted in an ultra-flat frame, barely 2.5 centimeters thick!

Boardman maximized the potential of this futuristic machine by winning the gold medal. The synergy between man and machine was evident. "Clearly, they [Lotus] spent their time working on it, and I put in my time and effort, and it worked well," he commented, celebrating the partnership with Lotus.

Detractors even suggested, quite openly, that it was the unobtanium machine that won the gold medal. To which the phlegmatic Brit later replied, "Everyone seemed to think I should be bothered, except me."

In working on the development of the Lotus Type 108, Chris Boardman kicked off five years of relentless technological innovation. In this arena, he had a worthy rival, another talented racer-inventor: Graeme Obree.

The Scotsman was Boardman's antithesis. Battling mental health issues, he struggled to fit into any team. He was a solitary amateur racer, broke, unemployed, tinkering with bikes in his garage. Without the benefit of engineers or wind tunnel tests like Boardman, he relied on his intuition and exceptional track sense.

Starting in 1993, Boardman and Obree engaged in a merciless rivalry. Records swung back and forth between them, sometimes multiple times within the same year! Like the Cold War arms race between the USSR and the USA, the two men embarked on a frantic pursuit of technological supremacy.

***

Up until the 1990s, the hour record was the exclusive domain of a select few extraordinary cyclists. Eddy Merckx set this benchmark in 1972 in Mexico, covering a distance of 49.43 km. Then, in 1984, Italian cyclist Francesco Moser, also in Mexico, shattered it twice within four days, reaching distances of 50.808 km and 51.151 km.

Moser utilized an aerodynamic bike featuring a sloping frame, equipped with bullhorn handlebars and a lenticular rear wheel.

Afterwards, the record seemed to fall by the wayside. No track cyclist appeared capable of surpassing it, and road cyclists, even the elite, steered clear. The required effort was daunting, and the potential for negative fallout in case of failure was a deterrent.

In 1993, Chris Boardman announced his intention to attempt to surpass Moser's eleven-year-old record, scheduling his try for July, post-Tour de France. However, Graeme Obree had a surprise in store...

While the cycling world's attention was fixed on the Tour de France, the Scotsman declared his own attempt at the record, shockingly set for July 16! This announcement was a complete surprise. "At the time, I was really upset," Chris Boardman recounts. "I had been prepping for six months for my attempt on July 23. I struggled with preparation and fundraising, and then, out of the blue, he breaks the record that was meant for me."

Obree chose the velodrome in Hamar, Norway for his attempt. On July 16, in front of just a few journalists and officials, he began his attempt.

Graeme rode a bike of his own creation, named Old Faithful. He ingeniously used a child's bike handlebar for its narrowness and a washing machine bearing for the crankset. There were even rumors that some frame parts were fashioned from metal scraps found roadside…

While Old Faithful's design raised eyebrows, the real shock came from Obree's revolutionary pedaling position. It was unlike anything seen before. He pedaled in an extreme forward crouch, nearly resting his chest on the handlebars, with arms wide apart. This position increased power but at the cost of comfort.

Despite adopting this unique "egg position" and riding a one-of-a-kind bike, Obree initially fell short, missing the record by nearly a kilometer.

Limited by finances, Obree had the velodrome booked for only 24 hours. After a night of drinking liters of water and minimal sleep (which he believed kept his muscles from stiffening), he attempted again on the 17th. Resuming the egg position, he this time managed to break the world hour record, covering 51.596 km—445 meters more than Moser.

Chris Boardman was initially livid. But his frustration was short-lived. On July 23, as planned, six days after Obree's attempt, Boardman took to the Bordeaux track. Riding an evolved version of the Lotus Type 108, still featuring a triathlete handlebar, he exacted his revenge, setting a new hour record of 52.270 km.

1993 proved to be an exhilarating year for track cycling enthusiasts! A month later, in August, the world's top track cyclists gathered in Hamar for the world championships. Graeme Obree emerged as the world champion in individual pursuit, while Boardman secured a bronze medal.

Obree's victory came with a bold declaration: he would once again challenge the hour record! His attempt on April 27, 1994, was triumphant, setting a new record of 52.713 km. In an effort to not lose even a fraction of a second, he even went as far as bolting his shoes to the pedals!

Following this, in May, the UCI banned the egg position. Nonetheless, in August, Obree attended the world championships in Palermo with Old Faithful. He competed with the same bike but was forced by new rules to adopt a more conventional posture.

He made it through the qualifications. However, the UCI interpreted some obscure paragraphs of the regulations in a peculiar way and decided to disqualify him. With his main rival seemingly the target of a scheme, The Professor had a clear path to win the world championship title.

At the end of the season, Obree also saw his hour record taken away, briefly by Indurain (53.040 km), and then by Rominger, who broke it twice (53.832 km and 55.291 km).

Certainly shaken but not deterred, the Scotsman showed his resilience and creativity. The story continued in 1995 in Bogota, at an altitude of 2600 meters. At the track world championships, Obree showed up this time with a more conventional bike, but equipped with exceptionally long aerobars. He appeared to be lying down on his bike. This stance was immediately dubbed the "Superman position."

Although his position elicited laughter, Graeme once again became world champion in individual pursuit. "When I saw that, I thought we were no longer doing the same sport. It wasn't cycling anymore but a machine propelled by man. But it was allowed, and I tried it," admits Boardman. "After three laps, I got it. Damn, it's so much better. We're going to have to use it."

At the Atlanta Olympics in 1996, Obree had to settle for an 11th place finish in individual pursuit. While this result didn't immortalize him, his famous "Superman" handlebars already had! Indeed, the gold medalist, Colinelli, used accessories directly inspired by the Scottish tinkerer's handlebars!

Obree, still an amateur, once again faced the professional world. But it proved to be a bitter failure. His mental state still didn't allow him to integrate with a team. He was fired before even racing a single race. Then, after a suspension for doping, he retired from cycling.

The path was now wide open for Boardman. On August 29, 1996, in Manchester, Chris would eclipse his former rival's achievements. At least, his results. Because his inventions, they lived on.

The Englishman showed up at the world pursuit championships with the famous "Superman" handlebars, which he claimed were inspired by those used by Colinelli… who himself had openly taken inspiration from Obree.

In the early qualification rounds, Boardman was scared. He struggled against Jens Lehmann. It seemed he was having trouble mastering his bike's trajectory, likely due to the "Superman" position. However, he didn't give up on it, convinced it would give him an undeniable advantage.

His gamble paid off. He quickly adapted to this new style and finished the qualifications by shattering the 4 km record (4 min 13 s 353). In Manchester, over two days, the benchmark time set by the last Olympic champion Colinelli was beaten eight times!

Chris Boardman found a formidable competitor in the Frenchman Francis Moreau. They took turns breaking each other's records. Back and forth, back and forth... until Moreau could no longer raise the bar. The Brit became world champion again and set the record at 4 min 11 s 114.

Nonetheless, he was openly skeptical about the multitude of recent innovations in track bikes. He felt it was going too far, especially since it was unclear where it would stop. He even stated that the "Superman" handlebar should never have been approved.

The UCI also recognized that this flurry of inventions was damaging the credibility of track cycling. With each new innovation, a record fell. The machine was overtaking human performance. The cycling organization had to put a stop to it.

But while waiting to legislate, the UCI still didn't veto the use of the famous handlebars created by Obree. And it was Boardman, his greatest rival, who benefited. On September 6, 1996, while the track of the Manchester velodrome was still warm, The Professor reclaimed the hour record from Tony Rominger by covering 56.375 km.

During this period, the Union Cycliste Internationale (UCI) members came together for discussions. They crafted the Lugano Charter aimed at curtailing the rampant technological escalation in the sport. Among its measures, it restricted the length of aerobars, effectively banning the "Superman" position and refocusing the sport on the athlete's capabilities.

Additionally, the organization ruled that recent track records would not be recognized as such. Instead, these times would be termed "best individual performances."

As a result, everyone was wiped from the record books – even Moser – and the hour record was officially reverted to Eddy Merckx. Though this didn't diminish Boardman's achievements, it was still a significant setback. And the onslaught of bad news didn't stop there.

In 1998, Boardman was faced with a far graver issue. Diagnosed with a form of osteoporosis, a condition that weakens bones, he found himself at a crossroads. The condition was treatable with testosterone therapy, but the UCI classified this hormone as a doping substance.

Faced with a harrowing choice, foregoing treatment meant risking serious long-term heart issues. However, accepting it could spell the end of his career. At just 30 years old and with plenty of sporting ambitions left, Boardman decided to delay the treatment. He wanted to conclude his career with a significant achievement: the time trial at the 2000 Sydney Olympics.

With the Olympics in September, the Tour de France, slated to be his last, was a crucial part of his prep. Yet, a sinus issue emerged just before the Tour, threatening to derail his plans. Despite his willingness to endure, Chris was advised against participating by his sports director, Roger Legeay, who made the tough call not to select him for the team.

Legeay's decision, though tough, was made with Boardman's best interest at heart, ensuring all team members were fully fit for the Tour.

In a moment of almost paternal guidance, Legeay challenged Boardman to return to the essence of cycling and attempt to break Merckx's record using the same equipment. Boardman, once a fervent innovator, agreed to revert to technology nearly 30 years old.

This challenge came as the UCI was looking to revive interest in the hour record. They agreed to officially recognize Boardman's attempt as a "record" if he could surpass Merckx, with the stipulation of using a traditional bike setup. Boardman accepted, further committing to not using an aerodynamic helmet for a truly old-school record attempt.

By July, Boardman began his meticulous preparation, understanding the significance of this challenge.

Come September in Sydney, he faced disappointment, finishing 11th in the time trial. With just one month until the record attempt, he had to push himself to extremes, enduring painful sessions on a bike modeled after 1970s technology. "Had I realized the pain involved, I wouldn't have pursued it. The position was unbearable," he would later confess.

On October 27, 2000, a back-pain-ridden Chris Boardman stepped onto the Manchester velodrome, his body a testament to the brutal training regimen of the preceding weeks. Yet, his determination was intact: "I'd really like to make a strong finish for my last race. It's symbolic since the hour record was my breakthrough."

As the race commenced, initial times were disappointing. Boardman was trailing Merckx's pace but intensified his effort, pushing through the pain.

His perseverance paid off, improving his situation, though the effort was agonizing. Past the 45-minute mark, the timing worsened, and Boardman struggled to generate additional power.

In the final laps, Boardman, driven to accomplish this feat, tapped into unknown reserves of strength, accelerating and sprinting the last stretches.

The clock stopped. Boardman had given his all. But had he covered the distance? Riding his "retro" bike, the Englishman managed 49.441 km, surpassing Merckx's 49.431 km by a mere 10 meters!

Boardman achieved the most astounding feat of his career by a slim 10 meters, equivalent to barely a pedal revolution! Hammered, in pain, but elated, he successfully completed his final challenge. He could now retire, content and proud, having fulfilled his duty.

Later reflecting on this achievement, he shared, "I was thirty-two, not at my peak, but I needed this record for my credibility. It was a way to clear the air and bid farewell."

A splendid farewell ceremony was held for the remarkable cyclist Chris Boardman. "Remarkable," a trait that distinguishes the true champions, much like humility. When asked nowadays if he believes he was one of the all-time greatest track cyclists, he simply replies, "I don't think I was better than others. I just found a niche and knew how to specialize in it."

And specialize in the pursuit of records he certainly did.

5

Fortune and Misfortune of A Scholar: Laurent Fignon

In the pelotons of the 1980s, Laurent Fignon stood out for several reasons. Firstly, even without intending to, his look made him instantly recognizable. He nobly sported a radiant blonde mane, initially tied back in a ponytail at the start of his career, which over the years thinned and became somewhat unruly.

He wore a tennis headband or a ponytail holder high on his forehead, insisting it was not for style but merely for convenience. Indeed, it takes considerable skill to remove one's glasses and wipe away sweat while gripping the handlebars.

For Fignon indeed wore glasses. A metal-rimmed model gave him the appearance of a scholar mounted on a bicycle. And this was not just for show; his extensive general knowledge and sharp intellect quickly earned him nicknames like "the Intellectual" or "the Professor."

Fignon was a complete cyclist, shining in both classics and stage races, remarkable in the mountains, quick in sprints, and comfortable in time trials. The man himself was wholehearted, honest, and could be temperamental. Some of his outbursts are legendary. That's how the public loved him. However, not everyone felt the same, as some figures in the cycling world did not appreciate his straightforwardness and occasionally sharp remarks.

Fignon's racing career experienced both towering highs and deep, dark lows. Each time, he emerged from the depths of the rankings to claim new victories and dazzle detractors and rivals with his talent.

Discovered young, he achieved early success. Yet, falls, injuries, and health issues did not spare him. "He never really had luck on his side," would say Cyrille Guimard later, who was his sports director for nine years and a close friend.

Their friendship began in 1981. Fignon, originally from Paris, was invited to the Tour de Corse that year. This unique race allowed the best amateurs to compete against professional cyclists. Performing well, Fignon caught the eye of Renault team's sports director, Cyrille Guimard, who soon signed him to a pro contract for the 1982 season.

With nearly fifty amateur victories, Fignon made an immediate impact. He won the Flèche Azuréenne, the Grand Prix de Cannes, and the Critérium International. Selected for the Giro d'Italia the same year, he made waves by temporarily taking the lead. His tenure in pink was brief – just a day – but it marked the start of a bittersweet relationship with the Giro.

Fignon nearly ended the 1982 season with a win at the Blois-Charleville classic. But bad luck intervened. Leading solo with a 40-second advantage 15 km from the finish, the Parisian suffered a rare mishap: his crankset broke. Caught off guard and unbalanced, he fell, tumbled to the ground, and saw Jean-Luc Vandenbroucke overtake him.

In 1983, like a fine wine, Laurent Fignon matured. He displayed serious prowess in the Tour of Spain. On the Vuelta's climbs, he was an outstanding teammate for Bernard Hinault, winning the fourth stage and finishing an impressive seventh overall.

With Hinault sidelined by knee pain, leaving the team without a leader on the eve of the Tour de France, Guimard entered a team without a clear leader, leaving the race wide open. Fignon, the premium teammate, naturally assumed Hinault's still-warm position as Renault's number one.

After a mixed start, it was in the Pyrenees where he laid the groundwork for a potential overall victory, moving up to second in the general classification. Then fortune finally turned in his favor, at the expense of the yellow jersey, Pascal Simon, who had to abandon after a crash on stage 17.

Inheriting the lead, Fignon fought hard in the Alps to maintain it. He cemented his final victory with a blistering individual time trial in Dijon. At 22, with his versatile skills, Fignon joined the exclusive club of riders who won the Tour de France on their first attempt. A prestigious group including Coppi, Anquetil, Gimondi, Merckx, and Hinault, his former teammate.

Unfortunately, his season ended abruptly in October with a wrist fracture from a fall.

With "the Badger" Bernard Hinault moving on, Fignon entered the following Giro d'Italia as the official and undisputed leader of the Renault team. That Giro was set to be his greatest frustration, not due to bad luck, unfortunate mishaps, or untimely injuries, but rather a shadowy collusion of figures from different backgrounds determined to see him lose. This led to a sordid saga in cycling, a nightmare come to life.

The 1984 Giro's prologue in Lucca was won by Italian Francesco Moser. The next day, Fignon took the "maglia rosa" after the team time trial, setting the stage for a showdown between the two. But Fignon was up against more than just a rider; he faced an entire nation and a biased race direction.

Moser, thought to be past his prime, had just won Milan-San Remo and broken the hour record in Mexico. Yet, he had never won the Giro, largely due to his struggles in the mountains. While capable of occasional brilliance on climbs, Fignon was clearly the superior climber.

In 1984, it was Moser's last chance to add the Giro to his palmarès, and it seemed preordained. He would be supported as much as possible by a united Italian front. Sometimes, national solidarity leads all riders from the same country in a peloton to collaborate temporarily to aid a compatriot. This was the case throughout this Giro. Almost no Italian rider dared overshadow Moser, a national icon, for fear of divine retribution.

The Giro's route that year was notably "flat," amusing some, given Moser's known difficulties in the mountains. Moser was destined to win this Giro, by any means necessary. And Laurent Fignon paid the price.

***

Returning to the race, Fignon managed to stay in the lead until the 5th stage, ending with the steep slopes over 8% of the Blockhaus della Majella. Moser, Fignon, and Argentin broke away together, each trying to gain an advantage. Unfortunately, the Frenchman suffered from a bonk in the final stretch, seemingly a hypoglycemic crisis. About 4 kilometers from the finish, he couldn't keep up with the pace set by the two Italians. He lost nearly 2 minutes to his rival and consequently had to give up the lead in the standings.

Francesco Moser held the first place for more than two weeks on a course that seemed tailor-made for him. If needed, he could count on the majority of Italian riders, regardless of their team, who would take up the chase if attacks became too threatening for him.

Only a few fellow countrymen, among the favorites, refused to participate in the charade. Mainly Roberto Visentini and, to a lesser extent, Moreno Argentin. They were crushed by the machinery. Visentini even drew the ire of spectators and was constantly heckled by the crowd lining the roads.

However, no one was fooled, and it was well understood that, as often happens, the Giro would be decided in the last days, on the Alpine summits. Laurent Fignon was biding his time. Moser knew it. So did Vincenzo Torriani.

Mr. Torriani was the director of the Giro d'Italia. He was well aware that the Frenchman could create a decisive gap in the Stelvio Pass. This summit in the Dolomites, reaching over 2700 meters in altitude, was the major challenge of this Giro. The day before stage 18, which theoretically connected Lecco to Merano via the Stelvio, Vincenzo Torriani decided to outright eliminate the pass from the stage!

The reason given was that the road was snowed in and therefore impassable. Faced with photos showing that the path was perfectly clear, he then cited avalanche risks. And he wouldn't change his decision.

Cyrille Guimard was bitter. "Okay, the Stelvio couldn't be done, but why didn't they plan another climb in its place?" he wondered, dismayed. His team lost a major opportunity to change the course of the race. Fignon, sarcastically laughing it off, quipped, "Are these mountain stages?"

Moser ultimately didn't lose any ground on what was supposed to be a terrible day for him. The standings remained unchanged. Laurent Fignon and Roberto Visentini, who had allied themselves, bitterly recounted the day's events. In addition to escaping the formidable Dolomite summit, their common adversary also benefited from unexpected help. Help that came from the caravan of motorcycles and follow cars…

Indeed, as they approached the Tonale, the two unfortunate companions launched an attack. "But when we dropped Francesco, the road between us was filled with cars and motorcycles," recounted Visentini. It was impossible for the duo of outsiders to properly execute their attack, while Moser, a few lengths behind, seemed to benefit from the slipstream of some interspersed vehicles. From the most commonly used to the most original, all means were fair to defend the first place.

Guimard was furious at the end of this 18th stage. He wanted to throw in the towel and abandon the Giro. But the team's sponsors, Renault and Elf, categorically refused. It was a matter of image. And then, according to representatives from both firms, the team's star rider still had every chance to make a difference in the five climbs of the 20th stage.

Before that, Laurent Fignon broke away from the field during the 19th stage. Unfortunately, a mechanical failure occurred, and his support car couldn't reach him quickly. He managed on his own. He made repairs as quickly as possible, got back on his bike, and managed to finish second, behind Marino Lejarreta. However, the time gained wasn't significant enough to take back the pink jersey.

The moment of truth, or so it was believed, arrived the next day. On June 8th, Fignon was all in. For him and his team, it was now or never.

And the Renault-Elf leader seized the opportunity! In the ascent of Pordoi, he left everyone behind, with the Dutchman Van der Velde in tow. They passed the Selle and then the Gardena together, but the Frenchman was too strong for his impromptu companion. He bags the Campolongo alone and finished the day's course solo, after a 50-kilometer breakaway. He had set the record straight. The pink jersey was his once again.

Behind him, Moser struggled. He held on with all his might but fell 1'31" behind Laurent Fignon. And it could have been worse, especially if he hadn't received numerous "boosts" from the frenzied tifosi lined up along the climbs. On several occasions, they sought to participate in their idol's triumph by giving him vigorous pushes under the saddle.

At the finish in Arabba, the hour record holder was devastated. He covered his pink jersey with a team jacket, not bothering to hide his disappointment. "I don't believe in miracles. I'm probably going to lose the Giro for the eleventh time, and by only a few seconds," he told the crowd of journalists surrounding him.

Laurent Fignon preferred to remain cautious, showing moderate joy. And he was right not to let his guard down. First, he was penalized 10 seconds for an illegal feed. Moser, on the other hand, was given a 5-second penalty for the multiple pushes that benefited him in this 20th stage. A rather symbolic punishment.

In the penultimate stage, the Italian gained 10 seconds for his third-place finish in the sprint. On the morning of the last stage, a 42 km individual time trial between Soave and the Roman amphitheater of Verona, the Parisian was ahead of his opponent by 1 minute and 21 seconds. "He can take a minute from me in the time trial, so I think I can win the Giro, Fignon declared, but I still need to be very cautious."

Cautious. Is he intimidated by the sporting threat that Moser poses? Or does he sense something else?

He would soon find out. The Italian arrived at the start of the time trial with his aerodynamic speed bike, equipped with a disc wheel. The race commissioners "did not oppose it." "Just before the start, when I saw him riding on his hour record bike, I realized it was probably over," Fignon recounted in 2009. "We calculated that the advantage of this equipment was two seconds per kilometer."

That advantage would turn out to be significantly underestimated. Francesco Moser set off before Laurent. This slight benefit, unfortunately, wouldn't be much help to the Frenchman. Hopes were high for a Fignon flash of brilliance, a moment of grace from nowhere. He did the impossible, pedaling like mad, but it wasn't nearly enough. Regardless of what anyone said, his rival was the hour record holder. And this short 42-kilometer distance was just a walk in the park for him.

As the amphitheater wasn't even in sight yet, spectators began the countdown. 3…2…1…0! The Frenchman's total race time had just exceeded Moser's. The Italian won his first Giro d'Italia at the age of 32.

Francesco indeed shattered the clock. He made up his deficit in the general classification and even added insult to injury. 1'03" ahead of the second-place finisher. An incredible average speed of 50.977 km/h. He quickly admitted that his modesty before the race was just a facade. His guru, Dr. Conconi, had indeed calculated that he could take back nearly 3 minutes from the leader.

The Renault-Elf leader was gracious after this "defeat," which was still a remarkable performance. "The result speaks for itself. I knew Moser was decisively gaining on me, and I went all out. Of course, I have regrets, but I lost against a champion who performed extraordinarily."

The calm of the usually fiery Laurent Fignon was only temporary. In the following days, he took up the issue again to denounce a final dirty trick by the Italian mutual understanding. He vehemently criticized the press helicopter that followed each rider during the last time trial. According to him, the positioning of this aircraft, flying anomalously low at certain points, was the cause of Moser's astronomical gain.

He would elaborate on his theory more extensively in 2004, in Procycling magazine: "You can see it in the footage. They're all low and behind him, so the helicopter's blades were pushing him. Then look at the photos of me, and they're all taken in front of me, so while the helicopter was pushing Moser, it was holding me back."

It may seem far-fetched. Just as much as the decisions of Vincenzo Torriani, who went out of his way to extract Francesco Moser from the grip that was inexorably tightening as the race progressed...

Decades later, Moser still defends himself from having received providential help from the helicopter: "The course went through urban areas where it was impossible to fly at low altitude. Plus, I was riding better than Fignon. In the prologue, I gained three seconds per kilometer."

"They knew I was capable of winning the Giro, and they made sure I lost," Fignon would declare, supported by Visentini, a collateral victim of the favoritism displayed for his compatriot: "I felt like it was a Giro that Moser had to win at all costs. And I wasn't wrong."

It was a journalist who covered the race, Gianpaolo Ormezzano, who later wrote a conclusion to this saga. A rough shell, but one that fits the facts perfectly: "Visentini, in good faith, always sees plots and ambushes. Moser, likewise, sees everything as normal and fair. The truth, not only in cycling, doesn't exist. And if there is a truth, it's relative to everyone."

Laurent Fignon, upset and even outraged by this injustice, was uncompromising. Shortly after, he arrived at the Tour de France as the reigning National Road Champion. He dominated the race. His climbing prowess wreaked havoc in the Alps, and the perfect unity of the Renault team was a precious asset in securing the final victory. His direct competitor—and former teammate—Bernard Hinault, finished second, more than 10 minutes behind.

The rest of his career was a roller coaster. Brilliant, even dazzling at times, the unfortunate Professor was not spared a myriad of physical setbacks.

After a strong start to the 1985 season, he injured his Achilles tendon by hitting one of his pedals. The surgery intended to treat this "beartrap" went well. However, he contracted a staph infection at the site of his wound, causing a permanent setback: a slight but irreversible loss of power in his left leg.

1986 started well, just like the previous year, with a victory in La Flèche Wallonne. Favored for the Vuelta, he "erred" during the 3rd stage. With a cracked rib causing him tremendous pain, he held on and finished in an honorable 7th place. The other big event of the year, the Tour de France, saw him face Bernard Hinault for the last time before Hinault's retirement. This time, it was pharyngitis that plagued the Parisian. Struggling like never before, he withdrew from the race on the morning of the 13th stage.

New respiratory problems—a sinus infection—hampered him at the start of the 1987 Vuelta. Despite a competition tailored for climbers, he lost too much time in the early stages and finished third in the race.

Another disappointment at the Tour de France. Fignon struggled and quickly saw his chances of victory slip away. Wisely, and very humbly, he then served as a super-domestique for Charly Mottet, one of the form riders of the moment. After wearing the yellow jersey, Mottet finished in a strong fourth place.

Entering the 1988 season, Laurent decided to breathe new life into his career by focusing on classics. And this new direction worked. In the iconic climb of the Poggio, he broke away with Italian Maurizio Fondriest and won the final sprint of Milan-San Remo. He also secured honorable placements in other classics, confirming a return to form.

But at the Tour de France, Fignon was unrecognizable. He was out of shape. Repeatedly, he fell far behind and sank into the middle of the pack. His poor form was explained when doctors discovered he had a tapeworm. Exhausted, he withdrew after the first mountain stage.

The champion magnificently emerged from the depths of the peloton at Milan-San Remo 1989. On the Cipressa, he followed Frans Maassen, who broke away. Laurent, more "supple" (as Guimard put it), then shook off the Dutchman on the Poggio climb. He crossed the finish line solo, achieving a historic double in the Primavera: he is the only Frenchman to have won this race twice.

After shunning the Giro since his 1984 misadventures, he eventually reconciled with the race. He aimed to win it. Fignon knew he had to crush the competition to avoid the same kind of debacle as in 1984. He worked diligently and finished the race proudly draped in pink. Pink, the color of his revenge. He joined two other cycling legends: Jacques Anquetil and Bernard Hinault. The only Frenchmen to have won the Giro.

Then came the Tour de France. Announced as one of the favorites, he once again savored stage victories on the Tour; and delighted in wearing the yellow jersey once more. The jersey became the prize in a fierce battle between him and the American LeMond. A legendary sporting duel, which ended tragically for Laurent. Hindered by saddle sores in the final days, he watched the race slip away by only 8 seconds, at the end of the last stage…

For a brief moment, he was the world's top-ranked rider according to the FICP, then the Parisian's career gradually declined. He won the Criterium International in 1990, then resisted the rising stars at the 1992 Tour de

France. But he increasingly felt outpaced by the growing power of the new generation of riders. His last trophy as a professional was the Tour of Mexico in 1993.

Becoming a TV commentator, Laurent Fignon commented on the Tour de France for the last time in 2010. The following month, after fighting courageously as was his way, he passed away on August 31, 2010, from metastatic cancer at just 50 years old.

A vivid memory remains of Laurent Fignon scolding the Giro director after his 1989 victory. As Torriani came to congratulate him, he bluntly said, "I'm sorry, but your Giro, it's crap."

A complete racer. And in every aspect, a complete man.

6

And For A Few Seconds More: Greg LeMond

In the backdrop of Laurent Fignon's career emerges another champion, discreet yet inseparable from Fignon's destiny: the American, Gregory James LeMond, or Greg to those close to him.

Both had promising amateur beginnings and were recruited by the Renault team in the early 1980s. Thus, they came from the same champion-making school led by Cyrille Guimard.

Quickly outgrowing their roles as Bernard Hinault's teammates, they were not content to be in anyone's shadow. Without even trying, they were thrust into the spotlight and onto the highest podiums.

Greg broke away from the Guimard-led Renault at the end of 1984, accepting a generous offer from the La Vie Claire team, headed by Bernard Tapie.

Hinault followed suit. Now wearing the same jersey but with a changed dynamic. Quickly, the American was no longer racing for his leader but alongside him, and sometimes, against him.

LeMond and Hinault teamed up for classics and more regularly in Grand Tours. Their age difference and respective forms tantalized the public. The almost fratricidal clash for the Tour de France between the two teammates at their peak didn't happen until 1986. Hinault's efforts were unrewarded as the balance tipped towards the American's youth, bringing the U.S. its first victory in the event.

Absent in 1987 and 1988, Greg LeMond made a comeback to the Tour in 1989. His former teammate, Laurent Fignon, dominated what the press dubbed "the craziest Tour." A suspense-filled storyline, twists and turns, and a wild, unexpected ending, delivered by a dream cast... A mythical moment in cycling unfolded that year, captivating fans for three weeks. Right down to the last seconds...

The lineup at the start of this Tour was arguably one of the most impressive the competition had ever seen.

Pedro Delgado, racing for Reynolds, had just won the Vuelta and claimed the 1988 Tour de France. He was a favorite to succeed himself. In his wake, his young teammate and compatriot, Miguel Indurain, quickly made a name for himself.

The Dutch Steven Rooks (PDM) and Erik Breukink (Panasonic-Isostar) were also contenders. Both had shone in the previous Tour edition, with Rooks as the best climber and second overall, and Breukink securing the white jersey as the best young rider, marking him as a serious outsider.

Ireland was represented by its stalwarts. The seasoned Sean Kelly was ready to disrupt the race, and Stephen Roche, the 1987 Tour de France-Giro double winner, was somewhat off his physical peak, leaving little chance for a standout performance unless by a miracle.

Attention also turned to one of Colombian cycling's pioneers, Luis Herrera of the Café de Colombia team, a formidable climber whose threat in mountain stages was undeniable.

A familiar face in the race, Laurent Fignon, a two-time winner in 1983 and 1984, was in top form and favored as one of the contenders. Also flying the French flag was the ambitious Charly Mottet, ranked number one in the FICP after victories at the Four Days of Dunkirk and the Criterium du Dauphiné Libéré, making him an outsider.

Lastly, American Greg LeMond, the 1986 Tour de France winner, rounded out this impressive array of cycling giants. However, he wasn't considered a favorite. Returning from a long recovery, he was more of an outsider.

The battle for the final victory was set to be fiercely contested. The stage was set for an unforgettable show. And indeed, it was a spectacle for the eyes!

The prologue, an individual time trial of less than eight kilometers in Luxembourg, was marked by an odd incident. Pedro Delgado forgot himself, arriving 2 minutes and 40 seconds late to the start ramp. This lapse in attention effectively dashed his hopes for a final victory.

Breukink won on July 1st. Close behind him, Kelly, LeMond, and Fignon finished tied for second, 6 seconds back, setting the stage for what was to come.

Delgado's troubles deepened the next day. In the team time trial, he fell off the pace completely, forcing his teammates to slow down and wait for him. Reynolds finished last, showing poorly.

The Belgian team ADR-Agrigel, with Greg LeMond, put up a strong showing, finishing 5th. But Fignon's Super U team was organized and efficient, winning the stage. However, the yellow jersey went to the Portuguese Acacio Da Silva, who won a half-stage run the same day.

He held the lead until the morning of the 5th stage. This 73 km individual time trial from Dinard to Rennes would be a tantalizing precursor to the rest of the race.

Pedro Delgado, due to his earlier poor performance, started quite early in the day and enjoyed favorable weather, setting the provisional best time. Charly Mottet, typically strong in time trials, wasn't in top form that day, leaving the Spaniard unbeatable for the moment.

LeMond appeared on a bike equipped with an innovative aerobar, already popular among triathletes. This new setup gave him an edge in aerodynamics. He outpaced Delgado by 24 seconds, even as the first drops of rain began to fall. When Fignon started later, he faced a torrential downpour.

Super U had also made modifications to their time trial bikes, but Fignon, not having had time to adjust to these new fittings, opted not to use them. He tackled the time trial with his standard bike. This cautious decision, compounded by the soaking wet roads, left him trailing the American by 56 seconds on the day. LeMond claimed the yellow jersey, setting the stage for an epic showdown.

The subsequent three stages across the western plains of France didn't shake up the overall standings. The first Pyrenean stage from Pau-Coterets to Cambasque showcased a rising star. Miguel Indurain broke away, leading over both the Aubisque and Bordères passes, and finished solo in

Cambasque. Pedro Delgado, trailing but vigilant, began his climb in the general classification. The rest of the race's heavy hitters played a game of cat and mouse, leaving Greg LeMond with a slim 5-second lead over Fignon.

The race's dynamics shifted dramatically in the 10th stage. With initial shots fired, the real battle commenced.

As the peloton tackled the first significant 20 kilometers of the stage to reach Luz-Saint-Sauveur, strategies began to unfold for the day's initial climb.

Pascal Richard from Helvetia launched an early attack. At the foot of the Tourmalet, a chase group formed, including Laudelino Cubino, Robert Millar, and Charly Mottet.

Cubino couldn't maintain the cadence and soon blew up, while the other two caught and passed Richard. Millar reached the inn just before the summit first. Behind, a vigorous chase ensued. A group of about fifteen riders, including the crème de la crème of the 1989 Tour and the yellow jersey, crested the summit 28 seconds later.

After a rejuvenating descent, Reynolds' Spanish rider Julián Gorospe broke away from the yellow jersey group, soon followed by his team leader Pedro Delgado. Delgado caught up with his teammate, then accelerated, leaving him behind at the start of the Aspin climb.

They quickly caught up with the race leaders. The defending champion, overcoming his earlier setbacks, was in fine form. He was a contender to defend his title but needed to excel to continue making up ground.

The trio led over Aspin, with Millar in front, holding a 2'17" lead over the yellow jersey group. Thanks to a well-navigated descent, the gap widened to 3'30", then to 4'45" at the base of Peyresourde, the day's third climb. At this point, Charly Mottet was the virtual "maillot jaune" holder.

In the final climb to Superbagnères, Delgado set a blistering pace. Two kilometers from the finish, he attacked again. Mottet cracked under the pressure and fell back, leaving the stage win to be contested by his breakaway companions. In the sprint, Millar secured the stage, but the real victor was Delgado, who continued his remarkable ascent in the standings.

Another showdown unfolded in the same location minutes later.

From the day's outset, LeMond, in yellow, found himself isolated within his group. Laurent Fignon, not at his peak, was determined not to give in. Pushed to the limit, the Frenchman even had to lead the chase when Rooks and Theunisse launched an attack in the final kilometers.

He couldn't catch the Dutch duo, but the increased pace put LeMond in difficulty. The American clung on with everything he had.

Just before the finish, Fignon made another move. LeMond countered by sticking to his wheel. Then, 500 meters from the line, the Super U leader attacked again. This time, Greg blew up. He lost 12 seconds to his direct rival and handed over both the yellow jersey and a 7-second advantage in the overall standings.

The Tour then traversed France from West to East, heading towards the Alps, but the competition's lead remained unchanged, despite an action-packed 13th stage on July 14th. Around 110 km in, Fignon and Mottet broke away. LeMond and Delgado were forced to pursue, eventually catching them. The day ended with a 100% French podium (in order: Barteau – Colotti – Gayant), and the favorites had to expend significant effort to maintain the status quo.

The Southern Alps set the stage for yet another shift in leadership. Stage 15, a 39 km individual uphill time trial from Gap to Orcières, saw Greg LeMond pull out his triathlon handlebar again, clocking the day's fifth-best time. The yellow jersey insisted on using the same bike and struggled to find his rhythm, finishing tenth, 1'44" behind the stage winner, and 47 seconds behind the American, who thus reclaimed the leader's jersey.

This stage left the race favorites frustrated and hinted at a thrilling Tour finish. LeMond was back in yellow, but his team was decimated, down to just four riders. And with only a 40-second lead.

Delgado hadn't made up as much time as he'd hoped and remained stuck in fourth place overall. Mottet, underperforming, posted the fourteenth-best time trial, yet held onto third place.

Conversely, PDM was all smiles, buoyed by renewed hope. Steven Rooks clocked the best time in the time trial, placing him sixth overall. At first glance, a final victory might seem out of reach for him, but considering his teammates finished sixth, seventh, and eighth on the day, and those teammates were none other than Kelly, Alcala, and Theunisse, anything seemed possible.

Indeed, everything remained up for grabs all the way to the Champs-Élysées. Especially with the majestic and mythical climb of Alpe d'Huez looming on the road to the capital.

Stage 17 kicked off in Briançon. The peloton first had to tackle the Col du Galibier and then the Col de la Croix-de-Fer before taking on the "road of 21 bends." And it was Gert-Jan Theunisse, unbridled, who made a splash. Breaking away in the Galibier with Viona and Biondi, the trio was caught by a group of eight chasers.

This newly formed group splintered on the climb to the Col de la Croix-de-Fer, but the Dutchman persevered and held strong. Alone, he faced about forty kilometers of flat to Bourg d'Oisans against a fierce headwind. He clung on, endured the pain, knowing he could make it to the end.

The remnants of the breakaway tried to close the gap. Yet, Theunisse held on and crossed the line solo, 1'04" ahead of the second-place rider. While everyone was impressed by the Dutchman's bold success, attention remained fixed on the battle for the general classification unfolding a few kilometers back.

As the race progressed towards Alpe d'Huez, the yellow jersey group dwindled. By mid-climb, only LeMond, Fignon, Rondón, supporting his leader Delgado, and Lejarreta remained. Lejarreta gradually fell back, and he wasn't the only one struggling.

Greg couldn't find a comfortable position, alternating rapidly between danseuse position and sitting. He was exhausted, visibly struggling. Cyrille Guimard, knowing LeMond well, urged Fignon to attack. Fignon hesitated at first, unwilling to risk a counterattack. However, he knew if he did nothing, he'd simply escort the ADR rider to the summit, allowing him to retain the coveted lead.

Guimard urged his leader to go on the offensive again. This time, he heeded the advice. He surged ahead, gaining a few meters on the group, but the American responded and stuck to his wheel. In a second attempt moments later, the Super U rider, who had spared no effort that day, gathered his last bits of energy and kicks again, with just 4 kilometers to go.

The yellow jersey wavered on his bike, struggling to stand. Powerless, "hitting the wall", he watched his direct rival surge ahead on the pedals, crossing the finish 12 seconds before him. Only Delgado, slightly fresher, managed to catch up with the Frenchman. The lead in the Tour changed hands once again.

Fignon solidified his lead the next day, finishing solo in Villard de Lans. With a strong finish, he gained an additional 24 seconds on his closest rival.

The final mountain day, from the Vercors station to Aix-les-Bains, saw a grouped arrival of the favorites. The battle for the stage win went to Greg LeMond, who outpowered his opponents in the sprint. A gracious Laurent Fignon congratulated him with a hug.

Stage 20, the last road stage, saw Sean Kelly securing a fourth green jersey, while the day belonged to the breakaway artists. The general classification remained largely unchanged. But trouble was brewing for Fignon. Since the day before, he had been silently suffering. His body was taxed after three weeks of racing, and inflammation from his shorts was causing serious discomfort.

Yet, he needed to persevere. His lead was comfortable at 50 seconds, with just one final time trial left. 24.5 km between Versailles and Paris. He knew the American was stronger against the clock, potentially able to reclaim 2 seconds per kilometer. But the Intello didn't see it as feasible.

He doubted LeMond could close the gap, a sentiment echoed by most race observers. This edition had already delivered enough twists and emotion. Everyone thought the outcome was decided, that the Tour would end quietly for Fignon after 24.5 km.

Greg LeMond, with nothing to lose, was determined to fight for every fraction of a second. He believed firmly, even if he was the only one. Even if it made him seem overly optimistic or even delusional. "It's possible, but it'll be close. I might win by one or two seconds," he said on TV the night before, in fluent French.

He brought out his triathlon handlebar-equipped bike again and gave clear instructions to his team: no intermediate times today. It was all about pure performance, pushing hard at every pedal stroke. To race like a Tour de France winner.

He shot out of Versailles at a sprinter's pace, delivering immense power from his thighs. Upon reaching the Champs-Élysées, commentators struggled to believe the incredible performance from the official outsider: an average of 54.51 km/h!

Still, the final result awaited, as Fignon's time, starting later, was unknown.

For the Frenchman, things didn't feel right. He seemed in trouble, his pedaling lacked smoothness, and he swayed from side to side. The clock confirmed these impressions. What seemed impossible was happening. He was indeed losing more than 2 seconds per kilometer to the American.

LeMond, already finished, anxiously watched the screens and the clock.

As the last kilometer approached, there was no longer any doubt. The situation had turned. Now, it was Fignon who needed a miracle to keep his yellow jersey. Promised victory seemed to slip away. He launched into a desperate sprint, while the cobblestones of the Champs-Élysées jolted his handlebars.

By the 200-meter mark, he was only 10 seconds behind LeMond. It was impossible to cover that distance in 10 seconds.

The moment Laurent Fignon reached the 100-meter mark, he lost the Tour de France. LeMond's time was better. The American, jubilant, had turned the Tour upside down with an extraordinary finish.

Fignon collapsed at the finish, surrounded by his team, sitting dazed on the ground. After racing a total of 87 hours and 38 minutes, he lost the yellow jersey by 8 seconds! Greg LeMond became the Tour winner by the smallest margin in history.

Moving to Team Z-Tommaso the following season, he confirmed his victory wasn't a fluke by winning again in 1989.

Unfortunately, by 1991, he couldn't keep up with the new generation of cyclists. He placed 7th in the 1991 Tour de France and claimed his last victory in 1992 with a win at the Tour du Pont.

The reason for the rapid decline of the star-spangled champion came in 1994 when he retired from professional racing to fight against the myopathy he was diagnosed with. This disease, which didn't develop by chance, originated a few years earlier.

***

In 1979, the young Californian was crowned junior world champion, kickstarting his professional career in 1981 at just 19 years old. He made history as the first American road world champion in 1983, and shortly thereafter, he also became the first American to stand on the podium of the Tour de France. Just three years later, he clinched his first victory in this prestigious race in 1986, a year marked by podium finishes and notable performances across Europe's celebrated races.

In 1987, a crash at the Tirreno-Adriatico resulted in a broken wrist for LeMond, sending him back home for recovery. On the verge of full recovery, his uncle and brother-in-law invited him for a hunting trip in the Californian countryside, meant as a leisurely escape. However, this outing turned tragic.

While hunting, Greg's brother-in-law shot at a bush, mistaking movement for game. Tragically, it was LeMond, who had not heard the call to fire, hidden in the bush.

He was struck by a shower of shotgun pellets in his back and side, collapsing and bleeding profusely. One of his lungs was severely damaged, along with other vital organs. Luckily, the nearest hospital had a helicopter, which was quickly sent to the scene. LeMond's life hung by a thread.

Surgeon Sandy Beal undertook a critical operation. With LeMond's life in serious danger, she managed to stabilize him, removing around 30 pellets from his body, riddled with shots. The remaining pellets would stay within him.

LeMond made a miraculous recovery, returning to cycling just two months after the accident, only to undergo another surgery. This left him severely weakened, with significant muscle loss, barely able to compete in short races before the winter of 1987.

At this low point, Bernard Tapie from La Vie Claire team, informed him of his dismissal with immense "class," via a letter.

Subsequently, the Dutch team PDM picked him up, but Greg struggled to find his former level. Further challenges emerged when his team directors informed him of a salary cut due to his underwhelming performances. Just another setback for him, now plagued by doubt and contemplating retirement. His title-less season in 1988 didn't offer much solace.

When it seemed all had lost faith in him, he seized an opportunity with the modest Belgian team ADR, led by Wilfried Reybrouck. Against all odds, LeMond's career soared anew, securing another road world championship title and, in that same year, an astonishing victory in the Tour de France.

The shotgun pellets that couldn't be removed led to lead poisoning, which subsequently caused the severe myopathy that led to his retirement. Despite a body battered and bearing the scars of his condition, Greg LeMond achieved a stunning return to competitive cycling. A phoenix rising, considering the medics in that helicopter had given him mere minutes to live.

This ordeal didn't just build a champion's mentality; it honed his insight, pragmatism, and realism. On the epic 1989 Tour, after the 15th stage to Orcières, he accurately predicted the race's endgame: "It's entirely possible I'll lose the yellow jersey and regain it. If, for instance, I'm a minute behind on Saturday, I could very well make up that time and secure the yellow jersey for good on Sunday on the Champs-Élysées. Who knows!"

7

The Lady on The Bicycle: Beryl Burton

The "Beryl Burton Gardens" is nestled in Morley, a small English town on the outskirts of Leeds. This memorial sits at the heart of the community, surrounded by buildings characteristic of the region. Access is through a narrow passage between two small buildings, under a wrought iron arch carrying a plaque with the name of the place.

There, a mural unfolds. An XL creation, over 18 meters wide. The late Beryl Burton, portrayed by local artists, is immortalized as everyone always remembered her: alone, bent over her bike, radiant in her sky blue and white Morley Cycling Club uniform. Nearby, a tribute to Burton, inscribed on a small blue plaque, begins with these words: "Beryl Burton OBE was a cycling phenomenon."

※

Her career, however, started later than most. At 20, she gave birth to her daughter Denise, who would follow in her footsteps, or rather, her bike trails. Barely back on her feet, she competed in the British Cycling

Championships for the first time, securing an impressive second place in the 100 miles and a sixth in the 25 miles. The event was dominated by Millie Robinson, the victor of the first Women's Tour de France in 1955.

Despite Robinson's clear superiority, Burton approached her after the race. With remarkable confidence for a newcomer on the national scene, she informed Robinson that next year, her performance would be significantly better. Direct, yet with quintessential British subtlety, she essentially promised her competitor future defeats.

The saying goes, "Easier said than done," but not for Burton who, by 1958, completely overshadowed Millie Robinson. True to her word, she shattered time trial records in the 25, 50, and 100 miles. Burton had ascended to the pinnacle of women's cycling, a position she maintained for decades. From 1957 to 1986 – highlighting her extraordinary longevity – she competed in 122 national championships, winning 73, mostly between 1958 and 1977.

She cherished the freedom felt in road cycling as much as the camaraderie of "parlor races," contested on velodromes. Inspired by her husband, also a cyclist who took up track time trialing, she discovered the discipline. The fearless Burton was hooked and decided to train for a major upcoming event: the inaugural Women's World Track Championships in 1959.

Already unstoppable on the road, she immediately asserted her dominance on the track that year. 1959 was a year of triumph. Hungry for recognition, she swept all major titles. A true blitz!

In her domestic championship, Burton clinched the road title and won the 25, 50, and 100 miles. There was nothing left for anyone else. On the track, she became, and remains, the first to win the World Championship in pursuit. The only blemish in her outstanding results was missing the World Road Title. But that didn't last long, as absolutely nothing and no one could withstand Mrs. Burton.

The following year, she achieved the "Grand Slam" by winning every major event she entered: the World Championships in pursuit and on the road, the British Championships on both track and road, and the time trials for 25, 50, and 100 miles. A clean sweep!

Her trophy haul continued for nearly three decades. Internationally, in track pursuit, Burton won the rainbow jersey five times (1959, 1960, 1962, 1963, and 1966), took silver three times (1961, 1964, and 1968), and bronze four times (1967, 1970, 1971, and 1973). Even when not winning, she was always a contender.

Her road racing record is equally unmatched, with two gold medals in 1960 and 1967, and a silver in 1961.

The road-track double in 1960 remains among the most unforgettable moments of her career. In the 3,000 meters pursuit final, she snatched victory from Belgian Marie-Thérèse Naessens while setting a world record. But more than the thrill of her first world titles, the standing ovation from 25,000 spectators in the packed velodrome would mark her for life.

Days later, Burton strapped into her pedals again to conquer the World Road Championships. On the Sachsenring circuit in front of more than 65,000 spectators, Beryl was in a league of her own.

After leading the pack for the first three laps, like a cat toying with its prey, she surged ahead in the fourth lap. No one could keep up. Absolutely no one could match her. Burton won by a staggering 3'38" gap from the peloton. Even the strongest male cyclists of the era struggled to perform better over similar distances.

Dominant in women's races, Beryl Burton enjoyed challenging her male counterparts whenever possible. In 1968, she requested to compete in the Grand Prix des Nations, a men-only event and a benchmark for individual time trials.

Her request was granted. Friends of the 31-year-old Brit pooled resources to cover her Leeds-Paris trip, marking her as the sole female cyclist ever to participate in one of the era's most prestigious races.

At the finish, Beryl was all smiles. Though her participation was unofficial, meaning she wasn't included in the final rankings, she did far more than just show up for a casual ride. She completed the 73.5 km Grand Prix des Nations at an average speed of 41.853 km/h, clocking in around 1 hour and 45 minutes.

For perspective, Felice Gimondi, the day's winner, covered the distance in 1 hour, 32 minutes, and 48 seconds, averaging 47.518 km/h. The last-place finisher, British cyclist Graham Webb, clocked 1 hour, 42 minutes, and 39 seconds. Burton's performance was comparable, proving she didn't come to Paris for a leisurely ride. With grace and a constant smile, she showed she could match the world's best male cyclists. It was during this appearance that Jean Bobet, brother of the legendary Louison, affectionately dubbed her "The Lady on the Bicycle."

Her participation in the Grand Prix des Nations remains symbolic, and despite her extraordinary effort, Beryl didn't outperform the lowest-ranked male cyclist. Against the best men, she fell just short... While she didn't disrupt male dominance this time, her exceptional event left a mark, where she intimidated the more modest riders and stole the spotlight from the best.

∗∗∗

A year prior, in September 1967, the Otley Cycling Club in England organized a twelve-hour time trial, open to all but divided into male and female categories.

The men raced first, with time trial specialist Mike McNamara, far from a novice, closing the men's event. Two minutes after his start, the women set off, with Beryl Burton the first to go.

Initially troubled by stomach pains, Burton eased her discomfort with a few drops of brandy. Freed from the nagging pain, she settled into her cruising pace, devouring the miles with astounding ease, as was her custom.

Approaching ten hours of racing, after covering 235 miles (about 378 km), Burton thought she was hallucinating. Who was this cyclist whose silhouette she spotted ahead? Surely, it was a straggler, not McNamara; he was too fast to have been caught. Yet, she needed to be sure.

She picked up her pace slightly and, as she gained ground, had to accept the reality: she was indeed catching up to one of the form men of the moment, Mike McNamara, and was about to overtake him.

Her daughter, Denise, recalls, "When she saw McNamara just ahead, she didn't know what to do. She almost panicked. But then she gathered herself, drew level with him, and offered him a licorice sweet. Then she resumed her pace, passed him, and left him behind."

After twelve hours of cycling, Burton totaled a distance of 445 km, averaging 37 km/h. Incredible! What the Leeds native had achieved was truly remarkable! With such a performance, she naturally shattered the women's 12-hour record. But more notably, by surpassing McNamara, she also broke the men's record!

The Englishwoman became the first – and only – woman to set a record in both male and female competitions under identical racing conditions. And to make the triumph complete and joyful, she outperformed Mike McNamara, a notable figure in British cycling at the time.

The men's record would be hers for two years before being surpassed. As for the women's 12-hour record, it would outlast her by decades! Indeed, it wasn't until 2017, fifty years later, that her British compatriot Alice Lethbridge improved upon her performance!

"Anything men can do, I can do," the Lady on the Bicycle would assert like a mantra. By managing to humble the best, she appeared otherworldly. Yet, her position of complete domination in cycling was far from preordained.

***

Born on May 12, 1937, Beryl Burton, née Charnock, came from a working-class family in Leeds. As a child, she was rushed to the hospital after losing consciousness for no apparent reason. The diagnosis was grim:

Beryl was suffering from Sydenham's chorea, coupled with acute rheumatic fever. The first condition is a nervous system infection that can be fatal.

Paralyzed on one side of her body, unable to speak, and suffering from sudden, uncontrollable muscle spasms, the unfortunate young girl spent 9 months in the hospital. This was followed by 15 months of convalescence in Southport, at a facility run by nuns, certainly one of her worst memories, as visits, even from close family members, were forbidden.

Recovered, after spending her twelfth birthday alone and away from her family, she was eventually declared on the road to recovery and sent home. Regarding her long stay in this medical facility, she later stated, "I felt like I had been deceived. I was determined to leave my mark in some way or another."

But at her age, there wasn't yet talk of quenching her thirst for life through sports, let alone cycling, nor of shaking up the world of women's cycling. After all, she would begin her passionate relationship with "the pedal" much later in life.

At 15, she left school and took a job in a textile factory, where she met her future husband, Charlie Burton. He would be a loving husband, completely devoted to his wife, accompanying her with quiet presence at every significant moment of her career. Advisor, caregiver, logistician, coach, the devoted Mr. Burton is undoubtedly the cornerstone of Beryl's career.

Not only her most diligent admirer, he was also the one who started it all. When Beryl and Charlie met, the young man was already a member of the Morley Road Club. One Sunday, he invited his sweetheart to watch a bike race. Seeing her evident interest in the "queen of sports," he suggested she come ride with the Morley Road Club on their outings.

The magic didn't happen immediately, far from it. Beryl enjoyed participating in the club's long rides throughout Yorkshire. But initially, cycling didn't treat her kindly. The beginner didn't sparkle and followed a steady progression to her most prestigious victories.

In her early days, the attentive Charlie had to push her up the surrounding hills. By her second year of practice, she was riding in the wake of the best local cyclists. Her husband recalls her third year: "She left us behind." The rest is history: she gave birth to her daughter, challenged Millie Robinson in 1957, and soon after, discovered the discipline of time trialing with Charlie.

As she wished after returning from Southport, she left her mark in history. The history of cycling. But she also impressed her contemporaries with her strong character and determination, traits common to all sports champions.

Aside from an insatiable thirst for victory, one wonders what inner fire drove Burton. What motivated her all those years, having elevated performance to a lifestyle? Because, as her biographer, Mr. Fotheringham, writes, "She was well-known but not many people really knew her."

Her closest ones are best placed to paint the most accurate portrait of the champion. Someone who lived her passion at every moment of her life. Someone who breathed cycling and, like a whirlwind, dragged those around her in her wake.

For her daughter Denise, "Cycling was our whole life. It was our main activity. We cycled for the social aspect as much as for the competition. I started being transported in a trailer before my parents gave me my first bike at 9 years old."

Immersed in the cycling world from birth, Denise Burton Cole would become a British champion and a world championship medalist, just like her mother. Undeniably, cycling runs in the Burton blood.

Jeffrey Charnock, meanwhile, seeks to nuance the image of a tough woman his sister sometimes projected: "People sometimes get Beryl wrong. They focus on how driven and determined she was – which she was. Or they portray her as very stern – which she could be. But there was so much more: she was kind and funny – not always intentionally – but she had a dry sense of humor. She was complex. Unique." And Denise adds, "She never stopped, she couldn't stop." Burton herself always said she "couldn't not try" and "slowing down would erode her self-discipline."

Self-discipline, certainly her most pronounced quality, propelled Beryl to the highest honors. Apart from her husband, who provided unwavering support, the Burton phenomenon never had any formal coaching or technical support of any kind, which adds another layer to her legendary tale. Another chapter that could be titled: "How extreme discipline allowed the Lady on the Bicycle to complete 25 miles in less than an hour, and 50 miles in less than two hours."

Decades after her career took off, when journalists asked if she reminisced about her beginnings, she said she didn't remember. And added, quite coldly, "What I remember is that I wasn't going to be beaten by anything." Is that sincere? Let's assume so, because false modesty and mind games were not her style.

Her uncompromising personality led her not to congratulate her daughter for her national time trial championship in 1976. That day, Denise finished ahead of her mother. But Beryl saw red and accused her of not playing the game. While Denise was crowned British champion, her mother left without a word. "I thought Denise hadn't done her job by not riding on the breakaway. Once again, I did the race. It wasn't sporting of her part. I can just say I wasn't myself at that moment."

A fierce competitor, whose integrity was never in question, Beryl owed her success to the strength of her powerful legs. No nepotism, no arrangements, no money involved. "All she wanted was to participate in events and win them. That's it," her daughter clarifies.

The Leeds native always made it a point not to earn money from her passion. Thus, her husband primarily sponsored her sporting adventures. She categorically refused enticing offers from prestigious sponsors, like Raleigh, even if it meant serious financial difficulties. "When you raced, you just prayed not to get a flat because you knew you didn't have enough money from next week's paycheck to buy a new tire. But I think if you really want to do something, you'll always find a way," she explained retrospectively in a 1994 interview.

After leaving her job at the textile factory, Burton got a job on a rhubarb farm. She maintained that her daily routine was the most effective training. She cycled to the farm, spent the day lifting heavy loads and digging the soil, then trained at night, hammering behind trucks on the roads around Morley. A determination that's nothing short of impressive.

For the 2010 World Time Trial Champion, Emma Pooley, her distinguished predecessor is a model of self-sacrifice. She highlights her selflessness: "Beryl never made a penny. On the contrary, her passion cost her money. I think her story should inspire people. She practiced sport for the love of sport, never thinking about money at any point."

Her stubbornness, which brought her a continuous flow of victories and recognition, would eventually turn against her. The Lady on the Bicycle tried to forget, to ignore the effects of the disease consuming her from within since her youth. Her heart was generous in effort. But the organ was also weakened by disease and quickly exhausted. She knew she risked her life by continuing to push her body to its limits as she did.

Defying doctors' advice, she continued to compete at the highest level from 1983 and, despite medical opinion, maintained vigorous activity until her death. She ignored warnings from a body in distress. She treated her body the same way she did her career: always higher, always stronger, always faster, even if it meant forcing the issue. But, like a race, not everything can be controlled, and external factors can upset certainties.

In 1996, just days before her 59th birthday, Beryl climbed on her bike to deliver invitations to her birthday party. Suddenly, the Lady collapsed. The emergency services did all they could, but the diagnosis was as brutal as it was cruel. The weary heart of the Lady on the Bicycle had stopped beating. Like Molière, who died on stage, Beryl Burton's life left her at the handlebars of her bike. She left her family without a true matriarch; her town of Morley without its brightest icon; and the cycling world without its proudest standard-bearer.

In 2014, the prologue of the 101st Tour de France started from Leeds. For the occasion, a play recounting Burton's life was performed at the West Yorkshire Playhouse. A tribute to the pioneer by the younger generation, as if to thank her, through her immense popularity, for revealing women's cycling to the world.

Already honored as a Member of the British Empire in 1964 and then as an Officer of the British Empire in 1968, the Lady on the Bicycle was inducted into the British Cycling Hall of Fame in 2009.

Beryl Burton elevated women's cycling to a higher level. Between emotion and admiration, it's our duty to salute the pioneers; those who went first. Burton's records challenged limiting beliefs; her performances changed perspectives on what could be achieved. And her story continues to inspire. For women and men alike.

8

Against All Odds: Freddy Maertens

Similar to Felice Gimondi (referenced in Chronicle 10), Freddy Maertens of Belgium shared his era with the legendary Eddy Merckx. Yet, the Flemish-born rider didn't exactly compete in the same arena as the Cannibal. His well-defined, powerful legs endowed him with a feared and formidable sprint speed. Known for his explosive strength, he was not only a master sprinter but also proficient in climbs and time trials. Maertens was the epitome of a complete sprinter with the capability to win titles.

However, following a stellar start, Freddy encountered severe obstacles, both professionally and personally. The career that had brought him fame and acknowledgment was also the source of his downfall.

Quickly dismissed as finished, the Flemish cyclist transitioned from obscurity back to the limelight for one last brilliant hurrah. Maertens' career trajectory was anything but ordinary, filled with turbulence and reminiscent of the gritty essence of classic cycling, complete with dramatic episodes, bold personalities, and various backroom deals. Battling against fate and adversity, Freddy Maertens developed a warrior's mindset, earning the moniker "The Comeback Kid."

※

Born on February 13, 1952, in Nieuwpoort, Belgium, Freddy grew up alongside his three brothers. It was his father who gifted him his first bicycle. Then, when Freddy won his first race, Gilbert Maertens agreed to buy him a higher-quality bike.

From that point on, Gilbert Maertens took complete control over his son's life, monitoring Freddy's every move. He knew exactly when and how long Freddy trained each week, watched for any dietary slip-ups, counted his hours of sleep, and knew who he was with and where he went. Nothing was allowed to interfere with the young man's progression.

In his quest for control, Gilbert went to extremes. Stubborn and possessive, he even sawed Freddy's racing bike in half the day he caught him flirting with a girl. Oddly, when Freddy was drafted for military service, his father intervened with the army to ensure no preferential treatment was given to Freddy.

This controlling relationship, sometimes conflictual, profoundly marked Freddy, affecting both his personal life and the early stages of his racing career.

Between 1966 and 1968, Maertens competed in races open to those without a license from the BWB, the Belgian cycling federation. He raced against competitors several years his senior and met who would become a teammate and friend: Michel Pollentier.

As a junior, competing against peers his age, Freddy started to stand out, winning about sixty races. Keen to tap into his cycling potential, the Belgian dropped out of school. His father allowed it, under one condition: unwavering commitment to training, regardless of the weather conditions.

Over the 1970 and 1971 seasons, he won around fifty races, the 1971 Belgian amateur road championship title, and a silver medal at the amateur road world championships.

At these same world championships, he narrowly missed first place. Closely watched by his father and raised in a culture focused on personal victory, the young man was deemed too individualistic by the members of the Belgian federation. Behind this politically correct excuse, Freddy paid a high price for his father's antics.

Gilbert Maertens, more vociferous than ever, had a strained relationship with the federation. He felt it was holding back his son's development. In 1972, he snubbed the federation's management and took over Freddy's training. Freddy, as usual, complied with his father's decision.

Despite a challenging temperament and impulsive decisions, Gilbert's tough approach yielded results. His son turned professional in 1972.

But as a counterpart to this minor consecration, Mr. Maertens Senior would heavily influence Freddy's early career choices. Before letting him "escape" into the professional world, he sought to take his share of the "time invested."

Indeed, the SCIC team offered to support Freddy in his transition to professional cycling, providing financial and material support for his last amateur season and an attractive contract for the following seasons.

Unfortunately, Gilbert had other plans for his son. He was already in contact with Pol Claeys, an industrialist and general manager of the Flandria team, and Briek Schotte, who managed the team with an iron fist.

To seal the contract, Claeys offered Gilbert a Flandria bicycle dealership under very favorable conditions. Freddy was thus pushed into the arms of the Belgian team, knowing it wasn't the best decision: "I would have preferred to go with SCIC and Colnago, but my father said, 'you have to do something for us too.'" He would learn the hard way that he had thrown himself into the mouth of a hungry wolf, close to its last penny.

From his first professional season, Maertens aimed to shake up the status quo. He had no intention of showing allegiance to the most experienced and prominent riders, such as Roger De Vlaeminck or King Eddy Merckx. Their emergence of this young upstart in the world of cycling was not welcomed warmly. However, journalists, tired of recounting Merckx's countless exploits, found a fresh story in the fiery young rider eager to upset the established order.

The rivalry between the Brussels native and the Nieuwpoort native would be exaggerated, deteriorating the relationship between the two riders. A portion of the public, captivated by Merckx's achievements, started to turn against Maertens.

The controversy of the 1973 World Championships would provide ample material for gossip columns, further dividing public opinion and fueling the feud between the two men.

On September 2, 1973, the two Belgian rivals were forced, for the first time, to cooperate. Wearing their national colors, they competed in the World Championships in Montjuich, Spain.

Merckx was at the top of his game, having swept almost all spring classics and clinching the Giro-Vuelta combo. Winning a third world title would allow him to equal Alfredo Binda and Rik Van Steenbergen. The idea appealed to him and tickled his ego. Maertens, equally proud, was honored by his first selection. He had one goal in mind: to make a strong showing in his debut with the national team. At 21, the Nieuwpoort native made it clear: he "wasn't about to ride for Merckx."

The first rider to complete seventeen laps of the 14.6 km circuit at Montjuich would be crowned world champion. From the start of the race, under the scorching Catalan sun, three teams took the lead: Italy, Spain (riding in front of their home crowd), and Belgium.

After covering more than 200 kilometers on a challenging course, the final showdown was set with three laps to go. Four contenders had broken away, riding together at the front: Felice Gimondi, Luis Ocaña, Eddy Merckx, and Freddy Maertens.

With two laps remaining, the Cannibal, undoubtedly the strongest of all, attacked and managed to pull ahead of his breakaway companions. He aimed to secure victory without waiting for the final meters, and the strategy seemed to work.

However, Merckx was surprised to see his compatriot Maertens suddenly appear behind him, alone. Unbeknownst to him, the young Belgian had just declared war. What was the rationale behind this counterattack? Did Freddy want to showcase his physical prowess? Aim for a Belgian one-two finish? Or more cynically, did he intend to put his teammate, who was also a rival, in difficulty?

Maertens always claimed he envisioned a Belgian one-two finish and would have let Merckx take first place. He insists that nothing else motivated his counterattack.

Intentionally or unintentionally, with the desire to secure second place or the urge to undermine his enemy, the young rookie changed the course of the race. Indeed, Ocaña and Gimondi used Maertens as a reference point. Following him, they increased their pace and managed to catch up with the two Belgians.

The Cannibal was furious. Just when he thought he had the race under control, his lieutenant had brought back two serious contenders who could snatch the title away at any moment. Deciding to reject any cooperation with Maertens for a joint victory, he initially refused. But he reconsidered, realizing it would be foolish not to take advantage of Maertens' sprinting ability, which he feared. He thus accepted the young rider's proposal.

As agreed, Maertens led the group while passing under the "flamme rouge", gradually accelerating. He constantly checked to ensure his leader was still on his wheel. So far, so good…

Approximately 200 meters from the line, Maertens unleashed his full power, convinced his leader was still behind him. In the heat of the moment, he failed to notice that the Cannibal had stalled, experiencing a massive loss of power.

The climax of the sprint unfolded in a fraction of a second. As Freddy prepared to move aside to let his leader pass in the last 100 meters, he glanced back and realized Merckx was trailing at the back of the quartet! For a brief moment, the shock destabilized him. Taking advantage of the situation, Felice Gimondi, finishing strong, overtook him on the inside to win by a hair's breadth.

For the Belgian camp, the finish was a disaster. Eddy Merckx, seething with rage, finished just off the podium. He blamed his junior for starting too soon and too strong. Maertens, unfazed, shifted all blame onto the Brussels native. According to him, the Cannibal should have signaled his weakness to free him from his mission and allow him to play his card in the sprint.

The two strong personalities exchanged harsh words. The elder felt sabotaged. A large portion of the public agreed and turned against the Belgian "rookie." Public opinion suggested Maertens should have wisely attempted to counter the attacks from Gimondi and Ocaña but should never have caught up with Merckx in the final kilometers.

The dispute between the two champions was definitively settled much later. In 2007, staying at the same hotel, the Walloon approached the Fleming: "Freddy, we need to talk about Barcelona," he said. "I think so too," responded the other. "We talked for three hours, shook hands, and it was all over."

Legend has it that, in reality, in 1973, the Fleming was collateral damage in the "brand war." At the time, the majority of the bunch rode Campagnolo-brand bikes. Only a few, including Maertens, used bikes from a brand trying to make a name for itself: Shimano.

With Eddy Merckx being a friend of Tullio Campagnolo, the founder of the eponymous brand, he allegedly refrained from informing his teammate about his weakness, simply to deny Shimano a major victory. He never confirmed this theory, thus fueling the legend.

The rivalry between the two riders became an integral part of their respective careers. Their adventures added to the long list of anecdotes and real or supposed dirty tricks associated with them.

In 1974, the world championships eluded Maertens again, falling into the hands of his greatest rival. However, according to the former, something not quite clear was orchestrated behind his back. He claims to have been poisoned, moreover by the entourage of his rival.

While Maertens led the race with Thévenet and Conti, he allegedly received a water bottle containing laxatives. Forced to abandon, he watched helplessly as Merckx was crowned.

According to Freddy, his masseur, Jef D'Hont, innocently acquired the water bottle from Gust Naessens, who was none other than... Eddy Merckx's masseur.

Naessens later confessed to the Nieuwpoort native. He recounts: "I got confirmation from Gust Naessens. I asked him, 'What did you do in Montreal?' Naessens replied, 'It's simple, Freddy. I was asked to give you a drink and I put something inside it. You were too good for my guy, so I added something inside to block you.'"

Like the rumors around the Campagnolo-Shimano war, no one has ever officially testified or stated anything publicly. Speculations will continue to fuel conversations for a long time.

Patience eventually pays off for Maertens. His perseverance finally bears fruit. Younger than Merckx, he takes advantage of the king's decline to ascend to his still-warm throne.

Freddy arrives at the 1976 World Championships in Ostuni, Italy, as the favorite and with the assurance of full support from the Belgian team. Eddy Merckx, still part of the team and unwilling to step aside, no longer has a say.

The Nieuwpoort native fully embraces his role as leader. At Ostuni, in the last lap, he catches up with a strong breakaway group, consisting of Yves Hézard, Francesco Moser, and Joop Zoetemelk, after a thrilling chase of nearly seven kilometers.

Afterward, he effortlessly counters two attacks from Moser, beating him easily in the sprint. After years of uneven battle against an almost invincible giant, Freddy savors this world-class title. Like many underdogs of that era, his performances were always deemed "honorable" against the gluttonous Eddy Merckx. But now, as the latter experiences the twilight of his career, those who lived in his shadow emerge. And Maertens is finally recognized for what he is: a highly talented complete sprinter and one of the fastest of his time.

Proof of this, nothing seems to stand in his way in 1976. In addition to the world champion title, he wins, among other achievements, the Belgian road championship, the Super Prestige Pernod, the Amstel Gold Race, the Grand Prix des Nations, and the points classification of the Tour de France. Maertens seems to breathe in the euphoria of victory fully.

To confirm his ascent to the pinnacle of world cycling, "The Comeback Kid" has an even crazier following season. 1977 is an excellent year for him, even though a few grains of sand, which became as many juicy anecdotes, slip into the machinery of his success.

Buoyed by his success in Paris-Nice, he is the marked man at the start of the Tour of Flanders two weeks later. This race will be at the center of a controversy that will generate a lot of ink.

※※※

The saga begins the night before the race when team leaders are summoned to a meeting by the race organizers. The aim is to highlight key regulatory points and officially announce any rule changes. Driessens, the sports director of Flandria, dismisses this as mere formality and pays scant attention. He overlooks a crucial update: the rules have changed. Previously, riders could swap bikes anywhere along the course. But from the 1977 edition onwards, changing bikes near the climbs is prohibited.

Barbé, "Lomme," seizes the earliest opportunity to leave the meeting and arranges for a backup bike for Maertens, to be placed at the foot of the Koppenberg, one of the stage's significant climbs. Driessens' oversight is a significant blunder!

On April 3, 1977, the race known as La Plus Belle Des Flandres kicks off in Saint-Nicolas. It's a grueling 260 kilometers, featuring steep ascents. Merckx, a frequent rival in Maertens' career, exemplifies resilience by breaking away early, over 100 km from the finish.

Merckx, "The Cannibal," is the first to conquer the Koppenberg, a mountain known for its narrow, deteriorating cobblestone path. With an average gradient of 11.6% and stretches at 22%, it's a formidable challenge.

Despite this, an elite group of Belgian cyclists mounts a fierce chase. Maertens, among this pack, switches his bike as planned before tackling the Koppenberg, unwittingly breaking the new rule. Oblivious to his infraction, he continues racing, heading straight for another regulatory faux pas.

On the steepest sections, Freddy gets a push from his friend, Marc Reybrouck. Reybrouck's assistance is so conspicuous that Maertens even passes other cyclists struggling up the slope. The charade ends when Walter Godefroot physically removes Reybrouck from the scene.

Temporarily, the boost helps. Maertens, unscathed by the climb, quickly distances his peers. He sets off after De Vlaeminck, who is in pursuit of Merckx.

"The Revenant" soon catches up with Roger, only for Roger to suffer a puncture. He falls a minute behind Maertens, who meanwhile, catches up with Merckx in the lead.

De Vlaeminck, in an extraordinary effort, manages to close the gap and joins the front group. But his strength wanes. He's pushed himself too hard, and a significant drop in energy threatens. The leading trio appears on the brink of collapse, but a sudden twist changes everything.

As the Flandria car reaches Maertens, they bear bad news: for changing his bike before the Koppenberg, Freddy is disqualified.

He contemplates quitting, but Driessens curtly advises him to press on: "Keep going, Freddy, it's good for the sponsor, and work it out with De Vlaeminck."

So, the two Belgians make a deal, especially as Merckx starts to fade and drops out at kilometer 212. From here, the accounts differ, with history offering alternative endings.

Maertens claims negotiations led to a hefty payout of 300,000 Belgian francs to lead De Vlaeminck to the finish, with half intended for Pollentier and Demeyer, his loyal teammates, and the other half for himself.

Roger, on the other hand, suggests they agreed on a simple gentleman's agreement for the next Paris-Roubaix, nothing more.

De Vlaeminck's subsequent visit to Maertens in Nieuport is recounted in detail by Freddy, who claims the Gypsy brought him money, but only half of what was promised to Pollentier and Demeyer. The remaining payment was never made, leaving the dispute unresolved.

Roger insists they never discussed money during their meeting. Similarly, Driessens denies proposing any financial arrangement, suggesting instead a reciprocal favor from the Faema rider.

This feud deeply scars Flemish cycling, with the two prominent figures attacking each other publicly through the media, each steadfastly holding their ground.

In 2011, a televised confrontation on "Canvas" shows neither has shifted from their stance, leaving the matter an open, painful wound. The true end of the story remains unknown...

***

Reflecting on the 1977 Tour of Flanders, it appeared a deal was struck between the two Belgian riders. Maertens rode the final 50 kilometers as if chased by the devil himself. His temporary ally regained some momentum, choosing to draft behind Maertens without taking the lead. On the brink of giving up, he suddenly found himself in a comfortable position to win.

With five kilometers to the finish, a dramatic twist occurred. Freddy learned that the jury had decided to requalify him, allowing his race results to stand. However, the news came too late. Exhausted from his effort, Maertens let Roger de Vlaeminck win without contesting a sprint, to the boos of the audience—a dismal turn for what was supposed to be a celebrated race.

The man from Nieuwpoort took revenge on fate at the Vuelta, satisfying his craving for recognition. Aided by loyal teammates Demeyer and Pollentier, and always fighting hard, he claimed the Tour of Spain, winning 13 out of 20 stages—a record that still stands.

Unfortunately, the tides turned abruptly. Freddy Maertens faced a storm. His world crumbled like a house of cards. In 1978, Flandria faced financial troubles, and he received only half his salary, paid in cash, off the books. The following year, he received no salary at all.

His investments, substantial earnings supposedly wisely placed, now needed to sustain him through hardships. To his dismay, most investments made in his name by those circling athletes turned out to be rotten. Other assets literally went up in smoke, like his furniture business, which disappeared in a fire. And, as the final domino fell, the Belgian tax authorities demanded a colossal backlog of taxes.

He and his family descended into hell. He plunged into severe depression. Suddenly earning nothing, he abandoned race after race. Known for occasionally adding champagne to his water bottle, he gradually succumbed to drinking.

Just before fully succumbing, the dethroned king rallied. It was too early to surrender. Briefly resurrecting his career, he returned to dazzle the pelotons and crush his rivals in sprints. This comeback was dedicated especially to his wife, Carine, who married him in 1973, despite others' disdain. Throughout the years, she supported him, even in the darkest hours.

"I must first thank my wife. She said, 'I'll handle the affairs, and you focus on being a professional cyclist.' I could set aside all my problems and dedicate myself entirely to cycling."

Freddy also owed thanks to his guru, Guillaume Driessens. His former sports director at Flandria, now with Boule d'Or, took him under his wing and awakened him from his slump. Maertens thus turned the page on his dark years at Flandria, harboring bitter resentment towards Pol Claeys: "He's not a good guy, he promised and promised and ..."

Between 1979 and 1980, Freddy won virtually nothing. He toiled in the shadows, suffering alone, aiming to return to his peak form. "By 1980, I felt it was getting better. I finished 6th in the Tour of Flanders, where I could have contested the final victory had I not crashed because of a child crossing the road. In the spring of 1981, I didn't finish many races. That was the plan. I trained in the morning. Then I'd race, abandon to train again behind a motorcycle in the evening."

His comeback took place in 1981, under the colors of his mentor's team, Boule d'Or. Winning a stage in the Tour of Andalusia and finishing 7th in Milan-San Remo, his return wasn't earth-shattering. He simply worked with focus and determination, preparing to strike where least expected: the Tour de France.

In the Tour, he won the first stage (or the first half-stage) and the third. The effort to rehabilitate his image was immense, but journalists mocked him. To them, this return was mere luck. "After the first win, and even the second, journalists wrote that I had been very lucky. The skepticism only disappeared after my third victory," he would recall.

Indeed, he accumulated victories, winning the 12th stage to Brussels and again the next day. Dressed in the green jersey of the points classification leader, he shone one last time by winning the final sprint on the Champs-Élysées.

Maertens had regained his champion form. One of history's greatest sprinters was back. On August 30, Freddy lined up at the start of the world championships. After two years of struggle, he dared to dream again.

In Prague, the circuit wasn't overly challenging. Slightly uphill with a few difficulties, it allowed for attacks.

The French attacked head-on, forcing the Italians to expose themselves to neutralize them. Then, 60 kilometers from the finish, a group of 31 riders broke away. Bernard Hinault, caught off guard, had to chase alone to join this group. Ismaël Lejarreta, joining the chase, didn't help by refusing to take turns. The Frenchman expended a lot of energy in the effort.

The lead group was forced to force the pace soon after. Sven-Åke Nilsson of Sweden had gone solo; the Italians led the chase and, with difficulty, caught him.

The day took its toll, and fatigue ultimately decided the race. In the last lap, Robert Millar attacked. Again, the Italians, acting as the race's pacesetters, sent Panizza, Baronchelli, and Contini to reel in the Brit.

In the final stretch, Moser led out Saronni for the sprint, while Maertens benefited from the excellent lead out of his compatriot Van Calster. In prime position, Freddy surged past the Italian in the final meters, securing one of cycling's most unlikely comebacks. The "Revenant" lived up to his nickname by becoming world champion for the second time!

Thus crowned, Maertens approached the next season. But it seemed his time had definitively passed. The brief revolt of a competitor stung in his pride quickly faded. From 1982, with the rainbow jersey on his shoulders, he went from crashes to abandonments. Mentally at rock bottom, he didn't even defend his title at the world championships, claiming injury from hitting his knee on a door...

The bottle gained the upper hand; unable to hide his weight gain, the Belgian was relegated to minor races he rarely finished.

Signed by second-tier teams seeking media stunts, Maertens competed in regional criteriums. The modest prizes he won went towards repaying his enormous debts. His wife, a true heroine, was the sole provider for the family, scraping by on odd jobs.

The Grand Prix of Hannut, won in 1983, was the last victory for the "Revenant." Then in 1987, after a training ride, he decided he no longer wanted to train in the harsh Belgian weather. Retiring almost unnoticed, Freddy Maertens stepped away from the spotlight.

After dominating the world of sprinting, achieving 142 victories, including 45 in the 1977 season alone (excluding criteriums), setting records in the Tour de France and the Tour of Spain, the fallen champion exited quietly.

Maertens went from the heights of success to the depths of despair overnight. He faced betrayals, lost public favor, and saw his personal life derail his career. Yet, he always found solace in his wife's unwavering loyalty through all trials. That might be his most prestigious victory. "Without her, we wouldn't be having this conversation. She's 90% responsible for my career successes, my comebacks, and my transition."

Would he do it all over again? Despite the hardships, for the thrill and exhilaration of success, Freddy Maertens would likely choose the same path.

9

The Irish Descent: Sean Kelly

"The Emerald Isle," Ireland, is celebrated for its lush, rolling landscapes and exceptional natural sites, like the renowned Giant's Causeway. And it's a giant of cycling we're discussing. A champion whose modesty matches the extent of his achievements, and who brought Irish cycling to the forefront in the 1980s and early 1990s.

Hailing from County Waterford in the south of the Republic of Ireland, Sean Kelly started cycling at 13, looking up to his brother. The following year, in 1970, he raced his first amateur race. He found his passion in cycling, and it reciprocated.

By 1972, at 16, he had clinched the Irish junior road cycling championship, repeating the feat the next year. Meanwhile, he supported himself working as a bricklayer.

Between 1973 and 1975, his burgeoning career was bolstered by stage wins at the Tour of Ireland and two Shay Elliott Memorial Races. The race, set on the steep hills of the Wicklow Mountains, hinted at the emerging champion's strengths: explosive in sprints, adept in descents, and capable in climbs.

In 1975, eyeing the Montreal Olympics, Kelly raced the Rapport Tour in South Africa. Amidst an international sports boycott, he competed under a pseudonym... but was uncovered. Punished by cycling authorities, he was barred from the Olympics.

Instead of heading to Canada, Kelly raced the Tour of Great Britain. There, he met Johnny Morris, a cycling enthusiast, who invited him to France for amateur races. The pay was modest: lodging, 25 pounds sterling per week, and 4 francs per kilometer for each race won.

While not lucrative, Kelly's performances were remarkable. Twenty-five races, eighteen wins. Jean de Gribaldy noticed and offered him his first professional contract in 1977 with his team, Flandria.

In March, he supported Freddy Maertens in Paris-Nice. At 20, he raced his first classic, a type of race he would excel in for the next fifteen years. He learned much from his Belgian teammate, who took a liking to him and taught him professional tricks.

Paris-Nice, the famous Race to the Sun, holds a special place for Sean. From 1982 to 1988, he dominated the event, winning seven consecutive years—a record yet to be broken.

His major breakthrough came in 1977, snatching victory in the 1st stage of the Tour de Romandie and finishing second in the Tour of the Netherlands.

Riding for Splendor from 1979 to 1981, Kelly began making a name for himself, despite the team's logistical struggles (Splendor sometimes withdrew from races due to the poor condition of their bikes!). Beyond numerous podium finishes, Kelly won several stages in the Tour de France and the Tour of Spain.

He ended the 1980 Vuelta with the blue jersey, awarded to the points classification winner. In the Tour de France, this jersey is green. A color synonymous with Kelly's native Ireland, fitting him perfectly. From 1982 to 1989, he won the Tour's green jersey four times.

His ascent continued in 1982 with Sem-France Loire, winning his first Paris-Nice. His race.

At that time, critics labeled Kelly merely a sprinter, incapable of winning stage races. He silenced them magnificently.

His potential soon exploded onto the cycling world stage. In autumn 1983, he won the Tour of Lombardy, his first "Monument" classic, edging out world champion Greg LeMond after battling through the Intelvi and Schignano climbs.

The following spring, Paris-Roubaix and Liège-Bastogne-Liège fell to him, along with a Tour of the Basque Country and a Tour of Catalonia later in the year. That summer, he placed fifth in the Tour de France. Kelly was insatiable, amassing thirty-three victories in 1984.

Kelly then rode a wave of success, a testament to his all-around capabilities, winning an astounding number of varied races. To name just a few highlights, he claimed two more Tours of Lombardy (1986 and 1991), two Milan-San Remos (1986 and 1992), a Paris-Roubaix (1986), a Liège-Bastogne-Liège (1989), two Tours of the Basque Country (1986 and 1987), and a Tour of Switzerland (1990).

His crowning achievement came in 1988, at the peak of his career. After winning his seventh consecutive Paris-Nice, he tackled the Tour of Spain. On a Vuelta with rolling terrain but without major mountain stages, he was second before the penultimate stage.

That stage, a time trial from Las Rozas to Collado Villalba, was Kelly's moment. He unleashed his power, overcoming a 21-second deficit to don the yellow jersey. The next day, in Madrid, Sean Kelly won the only Grand Tour of his career.

Kelly's career stands among the greatest in cycling. Considering total career ranking points, he is the second-best cyclist in history, behind only Eddy Merckx. And, for those in doubt, it's worth noting he topped the FICP rankings for five consecutive years, from 1984 to 1988, a feat unmatched to this day.

After physical setbacks in the early 1990s and before retiring in 1994, Kelly claimed his last significant classic in 1992.

On March 21, 1992, under sunny skies, 219 riders set off from Milan to San Remo, covering 294 kilometers.

The race started with several unsuccessful attacks until Fabrizio Convalle broke away solo. Claudio Chiappucci and Moreno Argentin, two favorites, led the peloton at a steady pace, giving the breakaway a lead of up to 21'50" before accelerating to catch him at kilometer 224.

Buckler's team then took the lead, maintaining the cadence over the Capo Mele and Capo Berta. Sean Kelly, now with Festina-Lotus, stayed hidden within the field, knowing well that "Milan-San Remo means waiting for your moment, conserving energy, and avoiding unnecessary exertion," as he described in his autobiography (Hunger).

Maurizio Fondriest was the first to attack on the Cipressa climb. Raúl Alcalá led the counter, overtaking Fondriest and soloing ahead. Alcalá, a strong climber, knew the race often hinges on the last 20 kilometers.

He crested the Cipressa with a 10-second lead, but Frans Maassen caught him on the descent. Together, they maintained a 15-second lead over a now-energized peloton.

Argentin then rallied his Ariostea teammates, who set a brisk pace, eventually catching Maassen and Alcalá as they hit the seafront, 3 km from the Poggio.

Eric Boyer briefly broke away, but Argentin quickly reeled him in. Argentin then launched several decisive attacks at the start of the Poggio climb, thinning out the competition.

The group narrowed to about fifteen riders, including Fondriest, Sorensen (working for Argentin), and Kelly in his Festina blue jersey.

As the descent to the finish began, Kelly made his move, asking his mechanics if his tires were securely glued. Assured they were, he felt confident to chase down Moreno Argentin.

Kelly's descent was a masterclass in speed and precision, pushing the limits of his tires' grip through the winding roads. "A bloc!"

Unable to follow, Sorensen and Fondriest watched as Kelly extended his lead. Argentin, fighting to keep every inch of lead in his home country, stayed low and tense, hoping to clinch the Primavera, a trophy missing from his collection.

With just over a kilometer left, television time checks showed Argentin 15 seconds ahead—a likely error, as Kelly caught him just before the "flamme rouge".

In a stunning turn, the race's favorite was overtaken by Kelly's lightning descent. As the crowd expressed their disappointment, the two exchanged words, setting the stage for the final sprint. Kelly was adamant about not taking a turn, "sitting in Moreno's wheels", saving his energy for the sprint.

In the final curve, Kelly surged past Argentin on the right, leaving him unable to respond.

As a crash took down part of the peloton behind them, Kelly crossed the finish line victorious, arms raised.

While cycling feats often occur on climbs, this time, a masterfully executed descent by the veteran from the Emerald Isle made the difference—an extraordinary feat for an extraordinary career like Sean Kelly's.

10

In The Shadow of A Giant: Felice Gimondi

Felice Gimondi's story is one of a cycling legend who reached the pinnacle of success at an incredibly young age. His journey is the kind many cyclists can only dream of. However, it unfolds like a tragicomedy, where he was set to dominate the cycling world but ended up having to carve out his existence in the shadow of the greatest cyclist of all time, Eddy Merckx. Merckx, known as "The Cannibal," captured all the attention, pushing Gimondi into a supporting role. But true to the spirit of a commedia dell'arte, the story has a happy ending. Bravo! The Italian ultimately triumphed over adversity, claiming spectacular victories that marked the zenith of his career.

Born amidst the turmoil of World War II, on September 29, 1942, in Sedrina, near Bergamo, Gimondi would grow to become one of the best cyclists of his generation and beyond. His pivotal moment came in 1963 when he won the Tour of Friuli Venezia Giulia, a race then only open to amateurs. This victory set the stage for a more significant breakthrough the following year at the Tour de l'Avenir 1964, competing against Lucien Aimar and opening the doors to the professional world.

The Italian team Salvarani was on the lookout for fresh talent and found Gimondi's all-around capabilities compelling. A superb climber and incredibly efficient in time trials, he could also morph into a formidable sprinter when needed, snatching crucial victories in the race's final moments. His integration into Salvarani in 1965 was a perfect match.

Gimondi didn't just step onto the professional scene; he burst in with vigor, claiming his glory without waiting for an invitation. Early in the season, he snagged second place at the Flèche Wallonne and landed on the Giro d'Italia podium (3rd). At the Grand Prix de Forli, Jacques Anquetil outperformed him in the time trial, but Gimondi's second place as a newcomer was impressive.

His ascent was rapid, seemingly unstoppable. His team took great care to nurture his talent, keen to protect his burgeoning career from burning out too soon. After showing promise at the Castrocaro Terme circuit, where the Grand Prix de Forli was held, Gimondi was supposed to rest at home. His sports director wanted to avoid overworking the rising star, deciding instead that Felice would watch Salvarani's Tour de France efforts from his couch in Bergamo.

But plans quickly unraveled as rider withdrawals mounted, thinning the ranks of those able to start the Tour de France. Just as Gimondi, still recovering from his duel with Anquetil and looking forward to some downtime, was set to leave for Bergamo, a call came. His sports director, Luciano Pezzi, informed him of another setback: Bruno Fantinato had injured his knee and was out of the Tour. Suddenly, Gimondi was drafted in as a last-minute replacement.

With the race starting in just two days from Cologne, heading towards Liège, Gimondi had no time to return home. Fate, in its generosity, had presented him with an incredible opportunity at the onset of his professional career. On June 22, 1965, as the peloton embarked from Cologne, Anquetil was noticeably absent, having decided to skip the Tour to recuperate for the rest of the season. With his main rival, Raymond Poulidor, viewed as the likely victor, the cycling world was astounded when Gimondi donned the yellow jersey by the 3rd stage. Initially, the consensus was that the favorites were merely letting the young rider enjoy his moment in the spotlight, expecting Poulidor to eventually assert his dominance.

Battling fatigue, Felice momentarily relinquished the overall lead to Bernard Van De Kerckhove but reclaimed it by the ninth stage. The cycling community was increasingly amazed at Gimondi's performance, especially as he appeared to be getting stronger. Despite this, there was a strong belief that the "natural order" would soon be reinstated, with Poulidor expected to effortlessly take control of the race.

During the ascent of Mount Ventoux, which the peloton is tackling for the first time, amidst oppressive heat, the anticipated scenario starts to unfold. With support from Jiménez, Raymond Poulidor launches an attack on the maillot jaune on the slopes of the "Bald Mountain." Felice hangs on but begins to weaken, inevitably. Poupou sets a blistering pace. The Italian starts to fall back; the gap increases. He's nearly at breaking point... when he suddenly finds a second wind. He's wearing the yellow jersey and is determined not to relinquish it. Although he keeps losing time to Poulidor, he dodges a complete meltdown. Fired up, drenched in sweat from his duel with the "Giant of Provence," battling fatigue and the doubters, Gimondi digs deep into seemingly far greater reserves than expected. At the finish line, despite a one-minute bonus, Poulidor can't claim the lead. He's 34 seconds behind Gimondi.

On the climb up Ventoux, Poupou appeared strong. Why couldn't he dominate or decisively end the race? Was he like a cat toying with its prey before the kill? Still, no one really believes in the "rookie's" potential victory. Despite surprising performances, the faith isn't there. No one sees Felice's full potential. The consensus is clear: Raymond will strike in the Alps and crush his rival in the upcoming time trials. His setback on Mount Ventoux will be just a footnote, and Gimondi's spirit will be praised, albeit with feigned modesty.

The plot proves wrong, and the script's predictions fail to materialize. The young sensation finishes the Alps with an increased lead over his prestigious challengers. With the audacity of youth, he even outpaces Poulidor in the final time trials. He never gives up the yellow jersey, arriving in Paris 2'40" ahead of second-place Raymond Poulidor. Standing alone, emerging as the champion he's becoming, Felice Gimondi clinches the Tour de France on his debut. He proves he's a force to be reckoned with, known for his love of battle and sharp tactical insight.

The following year, everyone expects cycling's new darling to confirm his elite status. But he surprises everyone. While he's less dominant in the Grand Tours, 1966 turns out to be a great year for him in the classics. He clinches victories in the Tour of Lombardy, Paris-Brussels, and Paris-Roubaix.

The Paris-Roubaix, rightfully nicknamed "Hell of the North" or even "The Toughest of the Tough," is more than just a classic race. This one-day event earns recognition for anyone who competes in it, and certain glory for the victor.

However, the flip side of glory is the promise of over six hours of suffering, battling either mud or dust. The Hell of the North originally spanned more than 250 kilometers from the Paris region to the "city of a thousand chimneys." Since 1966, the race, also known as the "Queen of the Classics," starts in Picardy. Divided into sectors, the course includes narrow, rocky passages through beet fields and sections of cobbled roads that wreak havoc on the peloton. These cobbled sectors, ranging from a few hundred meters to several kilometers in length, are notoriously difficult to navigate. Some, like the Mons-en-Pévèle or the Carrefour de l'Arbre sectors, have become legendary over the years. The total distance covered on these cobbled roads varies between 35 and 50 kilometers, with the course changing annually.

These cobblestones are irregular and can be incredibly slippery when wet. Each of these small blocks paving the way to the final victory can easily puncture a tire or warp a rim. Every sector, with its thousands of unique stones, can frustrate the most precise and robust mechanics in the world.

The Hell of the North is a formidable challenge for every participant, even the toughest competitors. During this lengthy classic, raced at a breakneck pace, cyclists must maintain high speed while navigating countless traps and obstacles laid out by the road. The accumulated fatigue, combined with the roughness of the surfaces, takes a heavy toll on the riders.

Strategy also plays a crucial role in conquering the Toughest of the Tough. Each team must employ tactics to protect their leader and keep him at the front of the race. With crashes, punctures, and mechanical failures being common, poor race management can mercilessly cost the victory, even for the most experienced.

Finally, individual technique is a key element that must be mastered. Riders need to become one with their bike, feeling their machine to push it to the limits of its grip without crashing. It's crucial to choose between riding in the center of the road – enduring constant, terrible jolts – or navigating the edges, which are more even but littered with massive obstacles and deep potholes.

Even though some of the now-legendary sectors weren't part of the Paris-Roubaix course in 1966, its layout was still incredibly demanding.

Among the champions and tough competitors at the start in Chantilly were Jan Janssen, Raymond Poulidor, Willy Planckaert, and Eddy Merckx, ready to tackle a completely new and unprecedented route.

On April 17, the sky is dark and low. Already shivering from cold and anxiety, the 137 starters are thoroughly drenched by rain showers. The start of the race is their first release. The time for hesitation is over. Now, they must strive to master this terrible classic.

During the race's early hours, the anticipated ordeal hits some harder than others. Stablinski wipes out, injuring his wrist, forcing him out of the race. Poulidor faces a series of setbacks: a crash, a puncture, and a mechanical failure, each time battling hard to catch up with the leaders. Even the press motorcycles aren't spared by the "Toughest of the Tough," with some timekeepers unusually ending up off course.

Belgian rider Maertens, avoiding these mishaps, decisively moves ahead. He breaks away from the pack and solos ahead, building up to a 4-minute lead. However, he's alone and perhaps moved too early, especially as he battles against terrible weather. At one point, he's forced to run up a hill with his bike, not from exhaustion, but from being chilled to the bone.

Maertens, later on, gets caught by another bold racer, Daniel Salmon. The Frenchman, also going solo, now faces the Paris-Roubaix challenge alone. He manages a slight lead over a quickly dwindling peloton, fighting against the cold, rain, and mud.

Surprisingly, as the race heads north, the weather somewhat improves. It's still freezing, but the rain stops. Jaak De Boever interprets this as a positive sign and makes his move. Near the first cobbled sections around Denain, he speeds up, scattering the previously tight peloton.

The Belgian from Wiel's quickly overtakes Maertens, then Salmon, taking the lead in this iconic race. Meanwhile, behind him, a young, vibrant underdog named Felice Gimondi, along with Michele Dancelli, breaks away from a rapidly thinning peloton.

The Italian duo rapidly catches up after a frantic twenty-kilometer chase, joining De Boever. Initially left behind, De Boever struggles but manages to keep up with the two Italians.

This trio works well together, consistently increasing their lead on the peloton. On the challenging and twisty course, their small group proves more efficient than a larger, bulkier one. However, any effort to organize a chase has limited success.

The attempt to catch up is disorganized. The strongest riders from a fragmented peloton form a group, including notable names like Poulidor, Godefroot, Van Looy, and world champion Janssen. Their efforts are disjointed, and Vittorio Adorni disrupts their rhythm even further by intentionally slowing the chase after his teammate Gimondi.

Despite the grueling conditions, Felice remains energized. He waits until 35 kilometers from the finish, then realizes he's in a league of his own compared to his breakaway companions. Deciding not to stick with them to the end, Gimondi ups the pace, quickly finding himself alone as Dancelli and De Boever can't keep up.

Illustrating his dominance, Gimondi extends his lead significantly over just 10 km, with the main peloton fast closing in on Dancelli and De Boever but still 2 minutes behind Gimondi. Through Péronne-en-Mélantois, Gimondi continues to push hard.

Riding nearly in his highest gear and smoothly handling the road's demands, he maintains a strong, rapid pace.

Approaching Bouvines, with just 19 km left and a brief easier stretch of road, the peloton hears Gimondi has extended his lead to 3 minutes. A group of strong sprinters makes one last coordinated effort to catch him, hoping for a sprint finish at the Roubaix velodrome.

Gimondi, however, is unstoppable. Despite the effort and harsh conditions, he navigates with unmatched focus, taking the best lines to maintain his lead. Using the cobbles, dirt strips, and even hedges for wind protection, he speeds towards victory with an average pace of 45 km/h, masterfully choosing the most navigable paths and cutting corners efficiently.

Near Hem, the escapee starts to feel anxious. He glances back several times, scanning for chasers but sees only motorcycles and support cars. No pursuers in sight. However, he has no idea how much time separates him from the main group. It's only after leaving the town that his team car catches up to inform him of his lead over the peloton: 3'45". Beyond his hopes.

His lucky star seems to shine brightly today. Perhaps it's due to the talisman he wears around his ankle? Earlier, during a visit to a miraculous cellar, Felice found a piece of string. Deeply devout, taking it as a divine gift, he had the string blessed by his village priest and tied it around his ankle. Undoubtedly, he feels the string brushing against his skin with every movement, keeping him in unwavering faith. In this hellish day, Gimondi knows who to thank.

The final challenge is the Beaumont hill. Situated 3.2 km from the finish, Poulidor had scouted this place for a potential "jackal trick" to avoid a sprint for the win. It would not be needed, as the Italian crosses it nearly 4 minutes ahead of him, with disarming ease.

After leaving Beaumont, the young Salvarani rider, quite pleased, leaves behind the cobbles. Still, utmost caution is necessary. Many riders, hit by sudden fatigue, have completely collapsed in the final kilometers, seeing their nearly written victories vanish. To avoid a dip in form and a crushing disappointment, Felice shifts to an easier gear.

As he approaches the Grand Boulevard leading to the Roubaix velodrome, victory is within grasp. And Felice is still hungry! He "shifts into high gear" by adjusting his gear ratio again, moves forward on his saddle, leans forward, and grips his handlebar tightly.

He zips up the artery like an arrow. Slowing down to tackle the last bend, he accelerates out of the curve and finally enters the velodrome. Only one lap of the track remains. 800 meters left under the cheers of the crowd.

Barely recognizable, covered in mud, with a thick layer of grime, Felice Gimondi crosses the line with a broad smile and raises his forearms towards the sky with difficulty. The performance is extraordinary. He completes the Paris-Roubaix in 6 hours, 59 minutes, and 26 seconds. And there is no one else in the picture.

Jan Janssen clinches second place in a sprint, finishing 4'08" behind. The gap between first and second is one of the largest ever recorded.

Interviewed by journalists immediately after the race, Felice Gimondi states that the 1966 Paris-Roubaix was one of his major goals. And even though he's extremely proud and happy to have won today, he reacts as if there was never any doubt about his victory. As if, for him, success was predestined.

The Italian public is looking for a new star, a successor to the Campionissimo, since Fausto Coppi retired. Given his 1966 performances, Felice Gimondi appears fully capable and ready. But crossing the gap from "mere" fame to becoming a legend in the sports pantheon is incredibly difficult. Only the greatest forever enter history and inscribe their names in gold. Gimondi will learn this, to his greatest despair, at his expense.

*
**

During the bountiful year of 1966, Felice Gimondi, affectionately nicknamed "the Aristocrat," won the Tour of Lombardy in a sprint, edging out a young rider three years his junior: Eddy Merckx.

As Merckx's career quickly ascended, the sporting rivalry between the Italian and the Belgian grew. To claim the status of the new

Campionissimo, Felice had to be unbeatable, relentless on his bike. He needed to dominate everyone, completely. And while Merckx was rapidly gaining strength, Gimondi stood firm against him, determined, his faith stronger than ever.

Between 1967 and 1969, the Aristocrat and the Cannibal were nearly matched. When Eddy won the first prize of the Super Prestige Pernod in 1968 and 1969, Felice closely followed in second place. While Gimondi won the Giro d'Italia in 1967 and 1969, Merckx took it in 1968 and 1970. For a while, the Bergamasco even gained the upper hand over his rival. After his victory in the Vuelta 1968, he became the second rider in history to have won all three Grand Tours, after Jacques Anquetil.

However, over time, the Cannibal inevitably surpassed him in this struggle. Despite Gimondi's exhaustive efforts, absolutely nothing and no one could counter Merckx's domination of global cycling. The Italian could only acknowledge his helplessness.

Against such a force of nature, in an increasingly uneven battle, Felice was relegated to the rank of eternal second. Second in the Giro d'Italia 1970, second in the World Championships 1971, second in the Tour de France 1972. Each time, Merckx was ahead. Yet, the Italian never faltered and continued to fight fiercely. But he was up against an opponent in prime form, winning nearly half of the races he entered, leaving only scraps for his rivals.

Gimondi still managed a few victories, like the Italian National Road Championship and the Tour of Catalonia in 1972. He had to make do with what the great white shark of cycling left for his competitors.

In his wake, the Belgian led a group of outsiders who, like a school of carnivorous fish, waited for any opportunity. Ocaña, R. de Vlaeminck, or Zoetemelk were also fierce competitors. They only occasionally rivaled the Cannibal, but they were ruthless whenever he didn't line up at the start of a race.

Caught between an unbeatable champion and a hungry younger generation, Gimondi's position wobbled. Many thought he was finished, never able to follow in Coppi's footsteps. It seemed his once-promising career had fizzled out.

Caught in a downward spiral, his morale hit rock bottom. Merckx's prime years were the worst moments of his career. Yet, like a smart and resilient competitor, he weathered the storm. He endured completely unjustified mockery, often from those who had never ridden a bike. And even if he flirted with the abyss during those years, he never succumbed to the sirens' call to give in.

Over the years, the Aristocrat learned to accept that he wasn't a bad rider; he was simply up against a much stronger opponent. Informed by his often unfortunate experiences, he learned to put things into perspective and let go. What else could he do against the one who would become the greatest rider of all time?

Out of these dark years emerged a new man, who knew how to distance himself even from the worst disappointments. Uninhibited and seeking the simple pleasure of riding, a transformed rider made his way back to the top, aiming to end his career on a high note.

In 1973, he made his comeback into the spotlight with a World Championship road title, along with victories in the Tours of Apulia, Piedmont, and Lombardy, topped with a Trofeo Baracchi.

The Milan-San Remo fell into his lap in 1974, along with numerous honorable placements in Grand Tours and classics. In 1976, the Aristocrat came full circle by winning his third Giro, while his eternal rival Merckx, no longer winning, finished 8th.

After a final season in 1977, ridden just for the pleasure of it, Felice Gimondi retired, the same year as the man who had dominated him for so long, Eddy Merckx.

Many tally Felice Gimondi's second places behind Merckx to construct a theoretical palmarès: "if the Cannibal hadn't been there…" However, it's time to shift the perspective and restore the Bergamasco as the main character of his own career. Once seen as Jacques Anquetil's designated successor, with six classic wins, five Grand Tour victories, and a 1973 World Championship, the Italian truly deserves his status as a great champion.

11

The Legend of The Green Giant: Erik Zabel

In the Tour de France, the points classification is a secondary ranking. Its leader is recognizable by the green jersey proudly worn on the roads of France. A widely held belief suggests that this green jersey rewards the best sprinter. However, such a simplification doesn't fully capture the essence of this competition.

The points classification was introduced to a still-evolving Tour de France. Following a scandal-ridden 1904 edition with various instances of cheating, race organizers decided to change how the general classification was determined. At one point at risk of disappearing, the Tour needed to preserve its credibility.

Thus, in 1905, the classification was established using a points system instead of time. Riders received points corresponding to their stage finishes, adjusted based on the time gap to the previous rider. The rider with the fewest points ranked first. In 1912, the race direction reverted to a time-based classification system, which remains in use today.

As the Tour celebrated its fiftieth anniversary in 1953, it was decided to reintroduce the points classification, but only as a secondary ranking. The ultimate winner would still be the one who completed the race in the shortest overall time and wore the yellow jersey.

The jersey awarded to the leader of this "secondary" classification was green, at the request of its sponsor, La Belle Jardinière. Contrary to what its name might suggest, this brand specialized in tailor-made clothing. The green color was simply part of its visual identity.

As with the original system, positions from each stage were added up, with the green jersey wearer being the one with the lowest number of points. However, from 1959, the scoring method changed. The first to finish earned the maximum points; those following earned progressively fewer points. The wearer of the green jersey was then the rider who accumulated the most points.

In 1966, intermediate sprints were introduced. These short bursts rewarded the first riders to pass significant difficulties scattered throughout a stage. Initially, intermediate sprints had their own classification. Though they also counted towards the green jersey, their value was diminished compared to points won at stage finishes. In 1989, this separate ranking was abolished, and points from intermediate sprints were integrated into the points classification.

Traditionally, more points for the green jersey are available on flat stages since the mountains have their own classification. Thus, road sprinters are most likely to claim the emerald tunic. This is why the green jersey is commonly thought of as the sprinter's reward.

In reality, the points classification honors the most consistent rider. It's not just about being the fastest. One must first finish the Tour and reach the Champs-Élysées. Then, it's about being part of the right breakaways, as well as finishing mountain stages within the time limits. It's no small feat...

***

Sprinter, strong rouleur, and resilient—these three attributes aptly describe Erik Zabel. The German, born in East Berlin, was so consistent that he even won the 2000 World Cup. His relationship with the Tour de France's green jersey is a long and beautiful love story...

The Zabel family has cycling in their blood. Erik's father, Detlef, was part of the GDR team competing in the Peace Race in 1955. Though he only finished ninth, he played a key role in helping Gustav-Adolf Schur win his first Three Capitals Race.

Erik was born on July 7, 1970, in East Berlin, at a time when the "Iron Curtain" kept half of Europe under wraps. As a junior in 1989, with his club TSC Berlin, he clinched his first significant title: a bronze medal at the GDR team pursuit championship.

This achievement was notable. In an era where sport served as a potent propaganda tool, excellent riders, trained rigorously and professionally, competed to gain attention and rewards.

Erik, who cut his teeth on East German velodromes, was part of the rising elite in a country on the decline. He exhibited all the qualities of an exceptional sprinter. His great capacity for work and focus would make him a professional renowned for his dedication and commitment.

In 1990, he won the last road cycling championship of a fading German Democratic Republic. He also featured in the GDR's national team at the Tour of the European Community for the last time. The young Berliner's reputation in East Germany continued to grow.

As Germany reunited, Zabel switched clubs, joining Olympia Dortmund. Quietly and unassumingly, he fanned the flames of a promising career. Crowned champion of North Rhine-Westphalia in 1991 and second in the German amateur championship the same year, he followed in his father's footsteps by competing in the Peace Race in 1992.

1992 was also the year of the Barcelona Olympics. Selected for the national team, Erik confirmed his excellent sprinting abilities by snatching fourth place in the road race. His career was ready to escalate to the professional cycling stage.

At 22, Team Union Fröndenberg served as a launchpad for his first professional season; enough time for him to be recognized and recruited by Deutsche Telekom. As the successor to "Team Stuttgart," the squad restructured and armed itself to become a powerhouse in the peloton.

One of the team's first major successes in the pink and white jersey was thanks to Zabel. In 1994, the Berliner won Paris-Tours, the first World Cup classic to fall both into his and Deutsche Telekom's lap.

The fate of Telekom and Erik became intertwined, following a similar trajectory. In 1995, Zabel claimed two victories at the Four Days of Dunkirk, two stage wins at the Tour de Suisse, and another two at the Tour de France. Nothing flamboyant yet, but Erik and his team were laying the groundwork for an unstoppable winning machine.

1996 marked the year of fulfillment. The German team made a decisive turn. With Riis, supported by Ullrich, aiming to win the Tour de France and deny Miguel Indurain his sixth title. More quietly, but just as effectively, Zabel won two stages and reached the Champs-Elysées in the green jersey. For the first time, the Berliner from Telekom clinched the points classification of the event.

1997 was even more thrilling. Zabel unleashed his irresistible power on Europe's roads. After winning the Tour of Andalusia, he easily triumphed at Milan-San Remo, rightfully recognized as the sprinters' classic.

Heading into the Tour de France full of confidence, Erik was determined to defend his green jersey. Early in the race, he temporarily ceded his jersey to Mario Cipollini, who accumulated leads in both the general and points classifications. The Italian enjoyed full support from his team, while Zabel had fewer teammates to rely on. That year, all eyes were on the gentleman's agreement between Telekom's leading men, Riis and Ullrich.

Winning the third stage, the Berliner seized the lead in the points classification, a position he held until the end. After claiming two more stage victories (the seventh and the eighth), he proved to everyone he was the most complete and consistent rider of the Tour.

He didn't stop there, maintaining his status for four additional consecutive years. In 1998, already the German champion, he also experienced the joy of wearing the yellow jersey. During the second stage, ending in Cork, while battling fiercely for the green jersey, Erik Zabel unexpectedly took the lead in the general classification for a brief day.

Just as unexpectedly, the sprinter took the lead in the points classification during the fifth stage. In Châteauroux, he finished second behind Mario

Cipollini. At the same time, the green jersey wearer, Ján Svorada, was relegated in the sprint for irregularity. Lying in wait, having bided his time, Zabel seized the emerald jersey.

As his teammate Ullrich battled for the yellow jersey amidst the turmoil surrounding the Festina affair, Erik steadily increased his lead over Svorada. Svorada's withdrawal during the 16th stage gave the German a significant breather, enabling him to finish the Tour in green.

After three consecutive years leading the points classification, Zabel had made the domain his own. Yet, at the start of the 1999 Tour, it was surprising not to see him on his throne.

The German sprinter found himself roughed up. The supersonic Mario Cipollini was the fastest. He swept all the sprint finishes in the early days. Estonian Jaan Kirsipuu, in his fight to keep the yellow jersey, also built up a comfortable lead in the points classification. And the unstoppable Tom Steels played the spoiler.

The situation eased after stage 9. Cipollini and Kirsipuu both withdrew on the same day, clearing the top of the points classification. Stuart O'Grady led, but the Berliner was close behind. Meticulously accruing points, Zabel grabbed the green jersey in Saint-Flour, the finish of stage 12.

Zabel managed to keep the industrious and dangerous O'Grady, a contender for the green jersey, at a reasonable distance. Although he didn't win any stages that year, Zabel, thanks to his exemplary consistency, once again won the points classification. That's four in a row!

Stuart O'Grady and Tom Steels returned the following year, joined by German Marcel Wüst to form a trio hungry for the green jersey. They eyed Zabel's success with envy, determined to shake the foundation he had built in the Tour de France.

Again, all three put the favorite for the green jersey through the wringer. Steels and Wüst won as many intermediate sprints as possible in the early stages. But once again, Erik demonstrated his incredible resilience. He wasn't there just to win the few flat stages at the start, only to disappear at the first sign of hills. And he proved it.

During the sixth stage, O'Grady was forced to withdraw after breaking his collarbone in a crash. But the German Wüst remained in contention. Worse, he was firmly installed as the leader of the points classification. It wasn't until stage twelve that a major upheaval occurred.

That morning, Wüst didn't start, and Steels abandoned early in the day. After much doubt about his ability to seize the green jersey once more, Erik Zabel found himself alone in the lead for the green jersey victory. With a gargantuan lead over Robbie McEwen, the runner-up, the Berliner was under no pressure. He won the sprint finish of the twentieth stage, the day before the arrival on the Champs-Élysées.

At this point in his career, the Berliner from Telekom had won the points classification of the Tour de France five times in a row. No one had done better. But could the humble Zabel win a sixth title? The competition seemed to be getting tougher, the contention fiercer. And without Wüst's withdrawal, it's uncertain if he could have clinched his fifth victory.

Erik would defend his title tooth and nail in 2001. He struggled mightily to overcome his rivals. Until the last moment, his title was in jeopardy, and one could even imagine witnessing the downfall of the green Giant in July!

The Tour got off to a great start for him as he clinched the first stage and instantly slipped into the green jersey. The next day saw Kirsipuu snatch the jersey, but Zabel reclaimed it the day after. However, mirroring Kirsipuu's strategy from 1999, O'Grady staged an impressive effort to hold onto the yellow jersey for as long as he could. He amassed a significant number of points, especially with his participation in a successful breakaway during the eighth stage. Occasionally leading in yellow, he also carved out a substantial lead in the points classification. And while he officially relinquished the yellow jersey after the tenth stage, he remained a formidable contender for the green jersey.

On the morning before the second-to-last stage, from Orleans to Evry, Stuart was still decked out in green. Erik, true to form, had been working systematically and with determination, inching closer to O'Grady in the standings day by day. Now closely trailing the Australian, the competition was far from over. He needed to outpace him, as history only remembers the victors.

Rising to the challenge, Zabel out-sprinted his rival to secure a third stage win. Yet, it wasn't enough to dethrone the Australian, who kept the fiercely contested "best sprinter's jersey" by a mere two points. Surprisingly, after more than 3,000 kilometers of racing, this slim margin kept the rivalry incredibly tight.

For the first time since 1996, the Berliner didn't approach the Champs-Elysées in green. Remaining philosophical before the start, he expressed no doubts about his ability to overturn the situation: "In the past years, securing the green jersey before the last stage was a given. But I enjoy this, the duel is thrilling, and it's great entertainment for the fans."

After two more intermediate sprints, Zabel was well-positioned to snatch victory near the iconic Arc de Triomphe. The task was daunting, as he had no teammates nearby to aid him, requiring him to fend for himself in pursuit of victory.

In the race's final moments, he maintained his position as Svorada unleashed his full speed. The Czech emerged as the fastest, unreachable by the rest. Yet, not far behind, Erik pushed hard for the win. Gripping his handlebars tightly, he seemed to pound his bike like a jackhammer, with O'Grady, who also had much at stake, right beside him, unleashing all his power to not lose ground to the German.

Unfortunately, O'Grady lacked a touch of speed, finishing third, just centimeters behind Erik Zabel. This narrow defeat and the few centimeters given up were costly. Sports can be unforgiving, as O'Grady found out, losing the green jersey in the race's final seconds to his Telekom rival, who left Paris with the points classification victory for the sixth consecutive year. However, this victory was hard-earned!

This victory, along with setting a new record, was the result of a relentless battle fought until the last second, marking it as a crowning success. Yet, it would be Zabel's last. In subsequent years, he finished second (2002 and 2006) and third (2003, 2004, 2007, and 2008) in the Tour de France points classification. With his momentum in France waning, the German shifted his focus abroad, to another Grand Tour.

In the 2002 Vuelta, he ended up in 69th place but won the points classification. He repeated this in 2003, finishing 72nd with a stage win, and in 2004, coming in 43rd while securing the blue jersey.

Despite facing media criticism and mockery, some calling him opportunistic and others questioning his sprinting prowess, Zabel's career was undeniably impressive.

Critics pointed out his reliance on rivals' withdrawals for some of his green jerseys, and some years, winning the jersey without a single stage victory, suggesting he was not a pure sprinter but a versatile rider. However, this versatility brought no dishonor.

Objectively, while Zabel might have lacked a bit of explosiveness compared to some sprint stars, his strategic reliance on his team's collective strength, able to form outstanding lead out train, showcased his racing smarts. The sprint isn't just about individual prowess; it's about team dynamics and strategy.

His so-called opportunism should be seen in the context of the green jersey's true meaning: it rewards consistency, not just raw speed.

Being a consistent and diligent rider is commendable. Besides winning the World Cup in 2000, his consistent performance elevated him to the number one spot in the UCI ranking in 2001 and 2002—a feat not easily achieved. His ability to stay at the forefront, ready to capitalize on any opportunity, underlines the essence of competitive racing.

Erik Zabel's achievements extend far beyond his victories in the points classifications at the Tour and the Vuelta. He also excelled in one-day races, effectively shutting down any doubters. He clinched three victories at Paris-Tours (1994, 2003, and 2005), a quintessential sprinters' showdown, and triumphed at the 2001 HEW Cyclassics, a premier event for the sprinting elite.

The Milan-San Remo, yet another sprinter's classic, was among his preferred battlegrounds. Zabel had a penchant for winning in flurries. Following his 1997 Primavera win, he dominated the classic through 2001. Holding four wins at the Italian classic, he narrowly missed a fifth in 2004, marking the gravest mistake of his career. On this occasion, pride got the better of him.

On March 20, 2004, the 95th Milan-San Remo was decided in a bunch sprint. In the final straightaway, Alessandro Petacchi led the charge. By taking the wind, he inadvertently shielded Zabel, who was poised for the perfect moment to make his move. The German swiftly moved out and passed the Italian on the right. It appeared almost too easy.

Near the finish line, with Petacchi and O'Grady unable to catch up, Erik made a critical error. He slowed down and raised his arms to celebrate what he thought was his fifth Primavera victory... not realizing Óscar Freire was about to outsmart him.

In a last-ditch effort, the Spaniard "threw" his bike forward in a final surge. Zabel, despite his wealth of experience, had made a beginner's mistake. One shouldn't count their chickens before they hatch...

The finish was so close that officials had to rely on a photo finish to declare the winner. After reviewing the footage, it was evident Freire had clinched it. By a slim margin, but a clear one, the Spaniard bested the German champion by about 15 centimeters in "his" race. Zabel would surely kick himself over that blunder.

In 2006, at the age of 36, the Berlin native secured a well-deserved silver medal at the World Championships, just behind Paolo Bettini. Then, two years later, after a storied career, he announced his retirement. He made his final appearances at the Münsterland Giro and Paris-Tours, the race that had first put him on the map, before hanging up his wheels.

True sprinter? Sprinter-rouleur? Versatile rider? How should Erik Zabel be classified? But more importantly, does it really matter if he fits neatly into a category? Even though Peter Sagan has broken his record for green jerseys at the Tour de France, the German remains a legend who claimed titles across the 20th and 21st centuries, bridging the second and third millennia. And while the significance of the green jersey is often misunderstood, he will always be remembered as the original "Green Giant" of cycling.

12

The Eagle of The Mountains: Federico Bahamontes

Alejandro Martín Bahamontes, born on July 9, 1928, in the Spanish province of Toledo, is better known by his nickname Federico, a name under which he would make history. His father, Julian, a road maintenance worker, had him apprenticed in carpentry early on, but Federico found little interest in the trade and instead took a job at a bicycle repair shop.

In 1946, he invested 150 pesetas in a second-hand bike, using it to make deliveries for Toledo's merchants. Some of these deliveries involved black market goods, prompting him to ride during the hottest part of the day when the Spanish Civil Guards were likely to be napping in the shade of trees. Federico relished the moments he accidentally woke them, leading to pursuits that he cleverly evaded with his swift accelerations, leaving the guards in tricorn hats far behind.

However, one day, the guards set a trap by blocking off a road completely. To avoid capture, Federico had no choice but to hide under a bridge, spending hours in muddy, stagnant water with only his nose above the surface to breathe. He managed to evade capture but returned home with a fever, sweating and vomiting, leading to a three-month bedridden recovery during which he lost all his hair. When it grew back, it was curly, earning him the nickname "Lettuce" during his first amateur cycling race in July 1947. Despite the unflattering nickname, he quickly silenced any scoffers by finishing second in that race and winning his first race the following month in Toledo.

By the late 1940s, as an amateur, Bahamontes began making a name for himself, especially at the Tour of Avila. Turning professional in 1952, he impressed by holding his own against, and sometimes even outperforming, the top professional cyclists, showcasing extraordinary climbing abilities that elevated the discipline to an art form.

His legend began to solidify in 1954, at 26 years old. In February, racing for Team Splendid, he surprised everyone by winning the Côte Mont-Agel race. The following month, he led over several mountain passes at the Grand Prix of Cannes and the Grand Prix of Monaco. Recognizing his potential, Julián Berrendero, the Spanish team's sports director, included him in the national squad for the Tour de France.

It's important to note that until the late 1950s, cycling races in Europe featured a mix of national and regional teams, as well as brand teams, with cyclists relatively free to negotiate contracts across these different types. For instance, in 1959, Bahamontes raced the Vuelta with Team Kas, the Tour de Suisse with Team Condor, and won the Tour de France with the Spanish national team. This system gradually phased out in the early 1960s, making way for brand teams with stable rosters.

In his first Tour de France in 1954, Bahamontes made an immediate impact. In the Pyrenees, he was the first to bag the summit of the Aubisque, enveloped in fog. He repeated this feat the next day at the Tourmalet but was overtaken in the descent by Bobet, Malléjac, and Bauvin. However, Bahamontes wasn't finished; pedaling circles, inghe surged ahead at Peyresourde, breaking away from the small leading group and securing more points in the mountain classification, although he couldn't maintain his lead in the descent, finishing the stage in second place.

His skillful escapes in the Massif Central and the Alps, particularly over the climbs of Romeyère, Bayard, Galibier, and La Faucille, solidified his status as the tour's premier climber. He dominated the mountain classification with 95 points, compared to the 53 points of Louison Bobet, that year's overall winner, and finished 25th in the general classification.

For the man from Toledo, scenarios similar to the 1954 Tour de France would recur in the following years. He would dominate the climbs of the Tour de France, earning the nickname "The Picador" for a time, praised for climbing like an angel. Federico won the Mountain Classification six times, in 1954, 1958, 1959, 1962, 1963, and 1964, though he only accumulated seven stage wins throughout his career.

Among his accolades is the prestigious overall victory at the 1959 Tour de France, a remarkable achievement, yet it remained his sole triumph. Despite two podium finishes (second in 1963 and third in 1964), he rarely managed to consistently challenge the favorites and wore the yellow jersey only on exceptional occasions.

His results in the Vuelta a España mirrored this pattern. In seven participations, he finished second once (1957), won two mountain classifications (1957 and 1958), and three stage victories, but never claimed the overall victory.

In the Giro d'Italia, Federico appeared only three times. The Giro was somewhat unfamiliar territory for him. In 1956, despite withdrawing, he still clinched the title of best climber. In 1958, he achieved his only stage win in the race and finished 17th. An injury forced him to withdraw again in 1961.

At first glance, given his robust health, extraordinary strength, and repeated mountain exploits, one might be puzzled by his relatively modest list of victories. While his record of leading over summits is impressive, the number of races he won is not as high as one might expect.

To understand this, one must delve into Federico Bahamontes' personality, as he was arguably one of the most eccentric and whimsical riders in the peloton. He was also a stubborn, unpredictable character with a fiery temperament, often struggling with moral dilemmas and lapses in motivation.

This "cocktail" of traits often detrimentally affected his performance. His volatile nature sometimes alienated his teammates, making it difficult for him to rally them to his cause.

Over his career, Bahamontes led over 52 mountain passes in the Tour de France, a record that remains unmatched. Yet, he was almost always caught in the descents that followed.

Known as "The Eagle of Toledo," he honed his skills on the poorly maintained Spanish roads, real "boulder gardens", which forced him to descend cautiously. This habit, however, cost him precious time on better roads when pursued by eager competitors, preventing him from capitalizing on his breakaways.

Anecdotes tell of a harrowing fall in the steep descent of Pajares during the 1956 Vuelta a España, where slipping towards a drop, he narrowly saved himself by grabbing onto a guardrail. This incident reportedly left him traumatized, unable to shake off the fear.

The almost divine aura of the best climber's title didn't help Federico focus his goals either. Being the king of the mountains in a Grand Tour was a highly esteemed honor at the time, guaranteeing invitations to various events throughout the year and substantial income, which was a significant incentive for Bahamontes.

He even went so far as to claim, perhaps mistakenly, that his contracts focused almost exclusively on winning the climber's jerseys, to the point where he would falter in flat stages. Often overcome by monotony during flat stages, he would sit up and voluntarily let himself fall back from the pack, simply out of boredom.

A story embedded in cycling mythology further illustrates Federico's aversion to anything that wasn't a climb.

In the 1954 Tour de France, the route for the first time tackled the Col de Romeyère in the Vercors region. Bahamontes, participating in his debut Tour, had already turned heads by leading over multiple Pyrenean passes. Then, during the stage from Grenoble to Lyon, he made waves again. Upon reaching the top of Romeyère well before the peloton, he made the unexpected decision to stop.

Legend has it he ordered an ice cream from a passing vendor and leisurely savored it while waiting for the other cyclists to catch up. It is confirmed that the Toledo native did indeed pause at the peak, and a vendor was present at Romeyère that day. Beyond this, fact and myth intertwine, reminiscent of Greek legends.

The specifics aren't entirely clear. At times, the main protagonist of this cycling caper claimed he was alone, but on other occasions, he mentioned being in a small group, though he's forgotten who they were.

Why did he stop, then? What led him to willingly dissolve his substantial lead? Only he could answer, and over the years, his explanations varied.

One of the reasons given by the "Eagle of Toledo" was a bear sighting on the Vercors slopes. Allegedly frozen with fear, he stopped rather than confront the animal alone.

Over time, in various interviews, he shifted his story to a mechanical issue—one of his wheels had several broken spokes. Unwilling to risk the descent in such a condition, he waited for his support car, which took a long while to arrive. To kill time, he reportedly indulged in an ice cream "with two scoops of vanilla."

Bahamontes also claimed, in a show of flamboyance to journalists, that he simply wanted to see who would crest the pass in second place. Alternatively, he seized the moment to reiterate that his aim was not stage victories but the best climber's jersey, making leading over Romeyère a goal unto itself.

About this incident, some believe the Spaniard knew the finish was too far to realistically aim for the stage win. Others, more critically, suggest that the future mountain king was apprehensive about descending alone...

Regarding Bahamontes and the ice cream, accounts also diverge. While witnesses confirmed a vendor's presence on the pass that day, what the cyclist consumed remains uncertain—even to Bahamontes himself!

He later reminisced about ordering an ice cream with two vanilla scoops. Then, contradicting himself in another tale, he claimed to have settled for a bottle of sparkling water. In further interviews, he asserted he merely asked the vendor to refill his bidon.

As memories blur and intertwine and witnesses fade away, Bahamontes cleverly plays into it. After building his career, he carves out a distinctive place in cycling lore.

The image of this eccentric rider, shaping his own enduring legacy, brings a smile. Yet, it prompts reflection on Federico's penchant for distraction, his tendency to lose sight of his main goals. His erratic mental game resulted in inconsistent performance. By undermining himself in certain stages, he seldom positioned himself to win races. These lapses peppered his career with highs and lows.

His stubbornness and impulsive nature notably led to his complete forfeiture of the 1960 Vuelta. In a protest against his teammate Julio San Emeterio's exclusion from the race, he intentionally fell behind the peloton and pedaled slowly during the fourteenth stage.

Berated by the crowd lining the roads, Federico almost comes to blows with a spectator who threatens him with an umbrella, while Bahamontes arms himself with a bike pump for defense. This altercation costs him nearly an hour.

Fed up, the champion withdraws from the race, which was enveloped in a toxic atmosphere. He claims stomach pains as the reason for his departure, officially. Unofficially, he criticizes the race organizers for failing to fulfill their responsibilities and showing too much favoritism towards certain competitors. The crowd turns against him, booing loudly, and the Spanish press lashes out, with the newspaper Arriba headlining, "The Eagle has Lost its Wings." Following the uproar, the Vuelta organizers decide to ban the Faema rider for 5 years.

In a similar spirit, the "Eagle of Toledo" shows up in top form at the start of the 1963 Tour de France. Despite being 35, the Spaniard is in excellent health. However, fixated on the title of best climber, he exhausts himself competing for this accolade, even though the overall victory is within his grasp.

In the peloton, everyone knows how easily Bahamontes can launch devastating accelerations in the mountains. All fear following his wheel when he breaks away, knowing that trying to keep pace with the "Eagle of Toledo" leads to inevitable burnout. The effort he puts into every pedal stroke is immense. Only a handful of excellent climbers and champions in their own right can challenge him in the mountains.

Among them are Luxembourg's Charly Gaul and the Frenchmen Raymond Poulidor and Jacques Anquetil, all starting the 1963 Tour. Unfortunately for him, Bahamontes fails to establish—or follow—a winning strategy. He could have stayed hidden within the bunch, then launched powerful, well-timed attacks that would have floored his rivals.

However, misguided, the Toledo native picks the wrong battle. He achieves new feats in the mountains, expending an excessive amount of energy. This excessive effort leaves him lacking the stamina to cement his dominance in the general classification.

Thus, during the 10th stage from Pau to Bagnères-de-Bigorre, Bahamontes starts pushing from the early kilometers. He's determined to catch a breakaway that has slim chances of success. He catches the escapees, then accelerates alone to lead over the Aubisque summit.

Caught later, Federico, driven by pride, pushes hard again. In the Tourmalet, his compatriot Esteban Martín attempts a break. Bahamontes catches him, followed by the race's other strong competitors. At the Tourmalet summit, it's Jacques Anquetil who wins the sprint. The Frenchman has perfectly managed the stage, letting his teammates work for him and attacking at the right moment. Bahamontes, on the other hand, lacks pragmatism, not as fresh as the Frenchman when it comes to the final sprint.

The next day, Federico again animates the stage too early. Along with a few breakaway companions, he manages to create a significant gap of 3'50" over the peloton, which includes Jacques Anquetil. He gains more points in the climbers' classification by leading over the Peyresourde pass. But at that moment, the breakaway disintegrates, with the finish still far ahead.

Uncertain how to proceed with Ignolin (Anquetil's teammate) at his side, Bahamontes slows down to wait for his teammate Mattio. By the time he catches up to his leader, the peloton has already accelerated. The two men are caught, and Federico finishes the stage in eighth place, 2'47" behind Guy Ignolin.

However, he does manage to win the stage from Saint-Étienne to Grenoble solo and even briefly wears the yellow jersey in the Alps. During the Grand-Saint-Bernard climb, Bahamontes attempts a solo escape. But caught, he has to contest the stage victory in a sprint against Anquetil. The Frenchman, once again managing his race better and conserving energy, defeats the Toledo native. Despite being the undisputed master of the mountains, Federico can't overtake Jacques Anquetil, who is more consistent and thoughtful.

The Frenchman, victorious in Paris, knows that Bahamontes was in better shape than ever. And that his bit of madness likely cost him the Tour de France. Geminiani, Anquetil's team director (Saint-Raphaël-Gitane), says, "With Jacques, we can go light candles and thank the Virgin Mary for this victory. Because if old Bahamontes hadn't played the young fool, the Tour was his without a problem."

The Tour eludes the "Eagle of Toledo" again the following year. He finishes on the podium, in third place, behind Poulidor and Anquetil. He could have done so much better... During stage 20, from Brive to Puy de Dôme, he breaks away with his compatriot from Kas, Julio Jiménez. Jiménez offers him a deal: if the Eagle gives up the mountain prize, he'll work for him. The lead they could gain should push Anquetil and Poulidor back enough to secure a victory in Paris for Bahamontes.

Federico flatly refuses the deal. Out of pride. It's unthinkable for him to let go of the best climber's title of the Tour, especially to a compatriot. So, no deal. Bahamontes wins his sixth Mountain Classification but forfeits the final victory of the Tour de France.

The resentment between Iberian cyclists is sometimes very strong in the 1960s. The country's political situation seeps into sports. Depending on the time or place, Bahamontes either channels the crowd's cheers or becomes the target of jeers.

This charged atmosphere frustrates the king of the mountains. And he's not one to back down. More than that, he lets no one dictate his actions. His strong character indeed stirs up quite a bit of turmoil within the teams he races for. His enmities and outbursts are etched in the history of cycling. His toxic relationship with teammate Jesús Loroño is a saga that captivates the public and fuels much discussion.

Harassed by the crowd along the roads, Federico almost ends up in a physical altercation with a spectator, who threatens him with an umbrella, while Bahamontes grabs a bicycle pump to defend himself. This confrontation nearly costs him an hour.

Exasperated, the champion withdraws from the race amidst a hostile atmosphere, officially citing stomach pains as his reason. Unofficially, he accuses the race organizers of failing in their duties and showing undue favoritism towards certain riders. Facing jeers from the public and harsh criticism from the Spanish press, with headlines like "The Eagle has Lost its Wings," the Vuelta organizers decide to ban the Faema rider for 5 years.

Heading into the 1963 Tour de France, the "Eagle of Toledo" appears stronger than ever, despite being 35. His obsession with the best climber's title, however, leads him to exhaust himself competing for this distinction, even when the overall victory seemed within reach.

In the peloton, Bahamontes' ability to launch devastating accelerations in the mountains is well-known. His rivals fear trying to keep pace with him, knowing it leads to their downfall. His intensity in each pedal stroke is enormous, with only a few top climbers and champions able to challenge him in the mountains.

This rivalry turns into an eight-year duel that taps into some of the deepest divisions of Spanish society at the time, regarded as the most intense rivalry between two individual athletes in the country's sports history.

During the 1957 Vuelta a España, the conflict between Loroño, Bahamontes, and their team director Luis Puig becomes the talk of the town. Their marked stances, altercations, and underhanded tactics dominate Spanish sports journalism.

Puig tries to play peacemaker in this bitter internal struggle. Loroño's more professional and measured behavior wins his favor, while he views Bahamontes as "uncontrollable."

Their conflict leads to ridiculous situations that undermine the Spanish team's unity in the tumultuous 1957 Vuelta. For example, once Loroño secures the red jersey, it's agreed he'll let Bahamontes break away to solidify his second place in the general classification and clinch the best climber's prize. However, suspicious, Loroño shadows Bahamontes at every attack, despite Puig's orders not to.

When Puig asks him yet again to back off, the Basque replies that he doesn't trust Bahamontes and prefers to keep a close watch. Bahamontes, frustrated by Loroño constantly catching up, breaks their agreement and increases the pace, enjoying the struggle it causes the team leader.

Puig also makes questionable tactical decisions during the 1958 Vuelta a España. Even though Bahamontes could potentially create significant gaps, his team director asks him to slow down for several days in a row to wait for Loroño, who can't keep up. This demotion to mere teammate status and the mandate to wait for Loroño is the last straw for the "Eagle of the Mountains," pushing him to the brink of his patience.

The tension between the two cyclists peaks during the latter part of the Vuelta, resorting to insults when riding side by side and flatly refusing to assist each other, regardless of the consequences. Ultimately, Stablinski benefits from the discord within the Spanish team to win the Vuelta a España.

The clashing personalities of Loroño and Bahamontes create a deep rift within the national team, pushing it to the verge of collapse. Bahamontes insists on being recognized as the team leader, Suarez refuses to support the Toledo native, and Manzaneque seeks independence. The team spirit disintegrates as each rider pushes their own agenda.

However, Loroño emerges as the biggest loser in these negotiations. He too demands to be the official leader of his team for the 1959 Tour de France but faces rejection from Dalmacio Langarica, the new team selector, who decisively cuts Jesús from the team.

Bahamontes, a polarizing figure, fosters and maintains animosity wherever he goes. During the San Sebastian stage of the 1960 Vuelta, his team, Faema, revolts against their leader, even chasing him down when he breaks away. "Faema shot me in the back," he states after the race. This time, Loroño, racing for Majestad, plays no part.

After a lengthy period marred by injuries and health issues, the "Eagle of Toledo" makes a comeback in 1962 with the French team Margnat-Paloma. The tensions among the Faema riders naturally dissolve.

Similarly, the opening of many events to brand teams prevents Federico and Jesús from having to coexist within the same squad too frequently.

While Federico's overwhelming personality smothers those around him (even the Margnat-Paloma team director, Raoul Remy, struggles to control him), he finds a mentor in someone he deeply respects. The only man able to channel his energy and, temporarily, tame his temperament is none other than the Italian Fausto Coppi. Coppi invites the Spaniard to lead his team, Tricofilina-Coppi, in 1959. Bahamontes holds him in high esteem, admiring his recent list of achievements.

Coppi pushes him to his limits, openly calling him "lazy" and a "shirker" without sparing his ego. Federico doesn't react; Coppi is the only one who can confront him with reality.

That same year, following this transformative encounter, Federico masterfully leads the Tour de France. Dominating the mountains as usual, Coppi's presence keeps his fiery temperament in check, forcing him to stay focused. Even benefiting from discord among French riders, he becomes the first Spaniard to win the Tour.

Unfortunately, with Coppi's death in 1960, the only person capable of restraining the volcanic Federico passes away, plunging him back into his old ways.

With a remarkable number of first ascents in mountain passes, Federico was named the "best climber in Tour history" by L'Équipe magazine in 2013. His record of six best climber titles would only be surpassed 40 years later by Richard Virenque.

Legend has it that during one of his last races, struggling Bahamontes kicks to escape the peloton's view, then hid in bushes, letting the peloton chase a phantom. Meanwhile, the "phantom" discreetly slipped into a broom wagon...

Myth? Reality? Whimsical, as they say!

13

The Flying Parisian: James Moore

Like Chris Boardman, James Moore was also a British subject and a record-setter in the cycling world. Just as "The Professor" was known for his innovations and contributions to advancing cycling, Moore was a trailblazer in his own right. A pioneer from a different era, another century, he made his mark for the first time over 120 years before Boardman, back in 1868.

Today's bicycle evolves more or less directly from the draisienne. This invention featured two wheels aligned and connected by a wooden frame. The rider sat on a seat mounted to this frame, with their hands on what resembled a handlebar, steering the whole setup with a lever system that directed the front wheel. Propulsion came solely from the rider's feet pushing off the ground.

The draisienne's creator, German Baron Karl von Drais (whose name inspired "draisienne"), showcased his invention's potential on June 12, 1817, by covering 14.4 km in an hour.

Marketed as the vélocipède in France and the hobby horse in England, the device quickly became popular across Europe. Yet, as progress marches on, the pedal-driven vélocipède emerged in the 1860s, gradually making the draisienne obsolete.

The major leap forward occurred in 1861. In Paris, locksmith and horse-drawn carriage repairer Pierre Michaud added cranks to the device after his son complained about the inefficiency of lifting his legs to propel his draisienne. These cranks, or pedals, were fitted onto the hub of the front wheel, on each side, and staggered by a half-turn. Thus, the vélocipède, once moved by foot propulsion, transformed into a pedal-driven vélocipède, now powered directly from the rider's feet to the front wheel.

It's worth noting, however, that Jean Lacou, a jack-of-all-trades, had ventured into similar territory well before Michaud. Fifteen years earlier, Lacou equipped a tricycle with a pedal system linked to a crankshaft, allowing it to move without foot pushing. He eventually discarded his invention, convinced it had no future...

Pierre Lallement from Lorraine, employed at a baby carriage factory, also claimed to have conceptualized adding pedals to a draisienne in the early 1860s.

Rumors suggest that German Philipp Moritz Fischer had the same idea as Pierre Michaud in 1853. However, Fischer did not formalize adding pedals to the front wheel, so the invention is often credited to the Parisian locksmith.

Michaud, unlike Fischer, capitalized on this discovery, further developed the pedal-driven vélocipède, and sought financial gain from it. He switched out the wooden frame for a cast-iron one, added an adjustable seat, and introduced a brake system. Moreover, he significantly increased the front wheel's diameter, understanding that a larger wheel would enhance speed due to the direct transmission of force to the front wheel's hub.

This led to the creation of the "michaudine," which also saw tremendous success. Eager to capitalize on this booming demand, Michaud expanded his production facilities by partnering with the Olivier brothers in 1868 for greater manufacturing capacity.

The partnership dissolved by 1869, and both parties ventured into more manageable business endeavors. However, as demand dwindled and fashion changed, Michaud père et fils faced bankruptcy in March 1870. The outbreak of war that same year definitively ended any hopes of a business revival.

***

Well before the debate over who first added pedals to the draisienne took hold, James Moore was born on January 14, 1849, in Bury Saint Edmunds, England. He was the eldest in a family that would eventually include eight children.

In 1853, James's father, a veterinarian by profession, decided to relocate his family to Paris. They settled in the Cité Godot-de-Mauroy, next door to a locksmith's workshop that specialized in carriages and tricycles: the Michaud workshop.

James quickly struck up a friendship with Ernest, one of Pierre Michaud's sons. The boys spent their free time in the local streets, mastering the art of riding the two-wheeled machines produced by the vélocipède factory.

Moore demonstrated an innate sense of balance and a fondness for navigating Paris's streets on these popular machines, often making trips to Maisons-Laffitte where his father ran a horse breeding operation.

The novelty of this mode of transport only grew, attracting more and more enthusiasts. This naturally led to comparisons of the distances each could travel. Some focused on achieving the longest distances possible, while others aimed to complete shorter distances at higher speeds. This burgeoning competitive spirit around the pedal-driven vélocipède led to the formation of clubs.

In 1868, James Moore became a member of one such group, the Véloce Club de Paris. On May 31 that year, in the Pré-Catelan gardens of Bois de Boulogne, he took part in his first competition, hosted by the Compagnie Parisienne. This event was a strategic move by Pierre Michaud and the Olivier brothers to stoke the growing enthusiasm for the vélocipède they produced.

Seven vélocipède racers went head to head officially for the first time before a crowd that had gathered along the course. The competition unfolded over a course of... 1200 meters!

Direct competition really appealed to James Moore. It was an opportunity to display his physical abilities and his finesse with the new two-wheeled device. He finished the 1200 meters first, clocking in at... 3 minutes and 50 seconds!

This event was long believed to be the very first bicycle race on record, with James Moore celebrated as the inaugural winner of such a competition.

However, recent findings by Japanese historian Keizo Kobayashi revealed that the first bicycle race actually took place about a year and a half earlier, on December 8, 1867. This race covered a 17-kilometer course from Paris to Versailles and featured around 150 cyclists, including politicians, artists, journalists, and both upper-class and working-class cyclists, many of whom were members of the Jockey Club.

The race kicked off at 9 a.m. from the Grand Palais, winding through the 8th and 16th districts of Paris, then Boulogne-Billancourt, Sèvres, and Chaville.

While Kobayashi couldn't pinpoint the winner, he established that the first three finishers completed the 17 kilometers in roughly an hour.

Even if the myth has been overtaken by reality, Moore's legacy remains undiminished. He soon participated in what is considered the first significant cycling epic.

This incredible story begins on October 20, 1869. The director of the newspaper Le Vélocipède Illustré, Richard Lesclide, aims to showcase the bicycle's practicality over walking. To prove his point, Lesclide organizes the first endurance bicycle race from Paris to Rouen.

In an announcement, Le Vélocipède Illustré invites "all velocemen from France and abroad" to participate, revealing the race's rules. Bicycles are welcome to compete, along with unicycles, tricycles, and quadricycles, as long as they are powered solely by the force of one man.

The race also stipulates that changing machines mid-route is prohibited. However, repairs are allowed, as is walking alongside one's bike. Participants are responsible for their own refreshments.

Initially set at 135 kilometers with four checkpoints, the course is shortened to 123 km just days before the event, with checkpoints at Saint-Germain-en-Laye, Mantes-la-Jolie, Vernon, and Pont-de-l'Arche. The distance must be covered within a maximum of 24 hours.

Registration is free and open to everyone, men and women alike. The first prize is a significant 1,000 francs—a considerable sum at the time (equivalent to a year's salary for an average worker). Participants finishing second through fifth will also receive prizes, and every rider who completes the course within the 24-hour limit will be awarded a commemorative bronze medal.

Furthermore, while everyone must register under their real name, competitors may race under a pseudonym or simply initials. Although cycling intrigues the public and excites its practitioners, it isn't very well-regarded by some segments of society. The Paris-Rouen race is seen as an opportunity to legitimize this activity.

The event records a total of 202 entries (323 according to some sources). On the day of the race, November 7, 1869, only 120 show up, including 10 foreigners and 6 women.

First, they must visit the headquarters of the Compagnie Parisienne, which also sponsors the event, to pick up their route card, which needs to be stamped at each checkpoint. Then they head to the Arc de Triomphe to await the start, scheduled for around 7:30 am.

A wide variety of machines, including prototypes, line up to compete, though vélocipèdes are the majority. In the cold, damp capital, on the brink of the Second Empire's twilight, picture this gathering of early cycles, quite unlike anything we're familiar with today.

The bicycles' wheels, made of wood and rimmed with iron like those of horse-drawn carriages, are quite large, nearly a meter in diameter. Some pioneers even experiment with replacing the iron with a rubber band, foreshadowing future pneumatic tires.

Pedals, attached to the hub of the front wheel, are sturdy levers that require significant effort to propel the vehicle. Each wheel rotation promises exertion for the bold rider.

Perched on a leather saddle, positioned far forward to reach the pedals, riders experience rudimentary comfort. This seat is mounted on a frame, generally forged from solid metal, evoking the robustness of old-fashioned carts.

The handlebar, crude in appearance, demands a strong grip and calloused hands. But strength isn't the only requirement for piloting a vélocipède of the time. Its handmade design also calls for a keen sense of balance to keep this machine, weighing over 30 kg, upright. And brakes are merely a luxury afforded by a privileged few.

*
**

The high society may have had mixed feelings about this novel way of getting around, but the general public was intrigued, thrilled, and eager to witness the inaugural endurance race. So much so that on the departure morning, around 7:15 am, an unexpected incident occurred.

Crowds had flocked to the vicinity of the Arc de Triomphe, with many clustering around a mutual betting booth set up for the event. As race participants continued to pour into the start area, a misunderstanding led a group of cyclists warming up away from the crowd to mistakenly believe the race had already begun.

Around forty competitors quickly mounted their bicycles and sped off toward Avenue de Neuilly. The racers who hadn't left yet voiced strong protests, yet race organizers opted not to disqualify those who had started early. Instead, they issued a second start 30 minutes later, with the understanding that this half-hour delay would be added to the early starters' final times, preserving the race's fairness.

By the 48-kilometer mark at the Mantes-la-Jolie checkpoint, Henri Pascaud was leading with a time of... 4 hours and 25 minutes! Close behind him was the English rider John Thomas, clocking in at 4 hours and 30 minutes. Shortly afterward, Pierre Bellay, James Moore, and Hinton Shand also checked in, having launched in the second wave and effectively bridging with the leaders.

Approximately 80 determined cyclists made it to the Mantes-la-Jolie checkpoint. Past this town in Yvelines, the race started to spread out. Jackson, on a quadricycle, dropped out at Bonnières. Truffault, not familiar with the area, got lost and wasted a significant amount of time before finally reaching Pont-de-l'Arche and stopping at an inn to refuel. There, he encountered Laumaillé, too spent to go on. Both opted to withdraw and took a train back to Paris.

In Vaudreuil, nestled in Normandy, a makeshift checkpoint was established to minimize cheating. After racing 98 kilometers, James Moore led the field. Castéra, Bobillier, and Pascaud followed in second, third, and fourth places, respectively.

The weather was unforgiving, with muddy roads that demanded extra effort from participants to push their mud-laden wheels. Some racers, including John Thomas Johnson, hit their first major wall of exhaustion.

Johnson's rescue came from the stationmaster of Vaudreuil, who, in a gesture of goodwill, quickly organized on-the-spot refreshments, making hot wine for the struggling cyclists.

As darkness descended, the members of the Veloce Club de Rouen, serving as the finish line judges, eagerly anticipated the first racer's arrival. Anxious to discover his identity, they crowded around him. "I am James Moore," announced the fatigued, sweaty, mud-splattered victor.

It was 6:10 pm. The Brit had just clinched victory in the first-ever endurance race between two cities! He completed the 123 kilometers in 10 hours and 40 minutes, managing an average speed of about 12 km/h.

At first glance, this pace might seem deceptively slow. Yet, it's vital to underscore that his machine lacked any form of gearing. One pedal turn equated to one wheel rotation, significantly amplifying the effort required. Even for a youngster barely 20 years old like Moore.

Castéra and Bobillier arrived fifteen minutes later and, in a display of good sportsmanship, agreed to be recorded as tying for second place, deciding to split the prizes for the second and third places. Hinton Shend, also refreshed by the Vaudreuil stationmaster, wasn't as fortunate. Just 7 kilometers from the finish, his bike broke, forcing him to complete the race on foot. He finished in ninth place.

Only one woman finished the race, placing 29th. She was an American racing under the pseudonym "Miss America," accompanying Mr. Turner, a bicycle manufacturer from across the Atlantic who had traveled to France for the event. She received a special prize for her perseverance.

The first tricycle, ridden by Mr. Tissier, made it to Rouen in the night, at 3:30 am, managing an average speed of just about 6 km/h across the race.

Of the 120 participants who set off from the Arc de Triomphe, only 32 made it to Rouen within the time limit. On the morning of November 8, the unfortunate Fortin was the 33rd and last to cross the finish line, at 8:30 am, outside the time limit.

Following this pioneering event, numerous races were organized. However, the burgeoning enthusiasm for what was becoming a sport was abruptly halted by the sounds of war. In 1870, the focus shifted to national defense, with French attention and resources understandably directed towards this cause.

During the Siege of Paris, James Moore served as a stretcher-bearer. After the conflict, he moved to London to pursue veterinary studies, following in his father's footsteps.

The UK hadn't experienced war on its soil, and Moore was both surprised and delighted to find that cycling had found its audience there too. Technology had continued to evolve, significantly improving bicycle performance.

Upon his return to his homeland, he participated in the first-ever British championship. He started strong and was in a good position to win but was prevented from doing so by a fall that resulted in serious head injuries.

The sport was quickly becoming international, with the world's best riders eager to compete against each other. In 1870, a landmark year, the first international race of significance was held at Molineux Grounds in Wolverhampton. James Moore, on a winning streak, clinched victory against some of the best racers of the time, like Keen or Shelton.

Originally the name of a hotel, Molineux in Wolverhampton became synonymous with cycling success as the hotel owner, M.O.E McGregor, began organizing races on his vast property in 1870.

As a savvy businessman, he quickly transformed a large portion of his property into one of the most significant cycling race venues. The best racers of the era competed there, drawing crowds of up to 20,000 people on some days.

M.O.E McGregor also inspired the creation of the McGregor Cup, considered the first cycling world championship. Between 1872 and 1877, the year he retired, James Moore won this race five times.

⁂

The story linking the British racer, the visionary hotelier, and the Molineux Grounds is also marked by a unique event: the first world hour record.

In 1873, James Moore, undoubtedly a man of many firsts, set himself the challenge to cover the greatest possible distance in one hour. He chose to stage this event at McGregor's estate, now transformed into a velodrome.

For this feat, he mounted a Starley Ariel 49. This machine bore little resemblance to the vélocipèdes that had rolled out of the Michaud factories years earlier.

James Starley had developed a model known as the "High Bicycle" in Great Britain, or "Grand Bi" in France. The transmission system remained unchanged; the pedals were still attached to the front wheel's hub.

To increase speed, manufacturers continued to significantly enlarge the front wheel's diameter. The "Grand Bi" Moore rode for his record boasted a 49-inch front wheel, hence the name Starley Ariel 49. This wheel, over 1.2 meters in diameter, had a gear development of 3.9 meters!

A ridiculously small rear wheel, with a section three times smaller, provided a semblance of balance for the cyclist. Perched about 1.3 meters high, the rider had little chance of a safe recovery in case of a fall.

Within an hour on a damp Molineux Ground, James Moore covered a distance of 14 miles and 880 yards, approximately 14.5 miles, or 23.331 km.

Thus, the first record was established. However, history seems hesitant to recognize James Moore as it perhaps should. Years later, as other athletes attempted to break the record, skepticism surrounded Moore's achievement. The announced distance of 14.5 miles was deemed too "neat," too perfect. It was suspected that the distance had been estimated or measured too imprecisely. As a result, the performance was deemed invalid.

The first accepted record was set by American Frank Dodds in 1876, who covered 16.471 miles (26.508 km). And the first officially recognized after the establishment of the ICA (International Cycling Association) was Henri Desgranges's in 1893, with 21.950 miles (35.325 km).

Fate seems to have been somewhat unkind to James Moore... Yet according to his contemporaries, he was indeed the best cyclist of his time. Hence, they affectionately dubbed him the "Flying Parisian," a nod to his French connections.

14

Return To The Summit: Alberto Contador

Alberto Contador stands among the cycling elite, having earned his victories through intense battles. He faced down formidable rivals, overcame health challenges, and navigated through disciplinary controversies, managing to claw his way back from the brink time and again to seize new wins, overturning scenarios that seemed set in stone.

Born in Pinto, just outside Madrid, Alberto Javier Contador Velasco began cycling as a pre-teen alongside his older brother, Fran. Initially, the bike was merely a quicker way to hang out with friends.

Without any particular ambition toward a professional cycling career, a coach spotted his unique talent. Somewhat unexpectedly, Alberto found himself enrolled at the Uni Pinto club.

As a junior, he moved to the Madrid-based RVC Portillo team. Contador kept a low profile, not immediately grabbing the spotlight but showing a distinct affinity for climbing. Despite his obvious skills, he was overlooked for the Spanish junior national team competing in the world championships.

This oversight worked out perfectly for Manolo Saiz, the manager of the Once-Eroski team, who saw something special in the young Alberto. Under Saiz, whom he came to regard as a second father, Contador joined the professional ranks of Once-Eroski in 2003.

His debut year surpassed all expectations. Contador quickly established himself. In August, by clinching the final stage of the Tour of Poland, he secured his first professional victory.

In 2004, just as his career was gaining momentum, Alberto experienced a serious crash during the Tour of Asturias, fracturing his jaw. But this injury was merely the tip of the iceberg.

While addressing this injury, doctors were shocked to find signs of an aneurysm rupture. This explained the convulsions that had caused his fall.

What unfolded next could have been lifted from a heart-wrenching novel—a narrative all too common where the promising career of a rising sports star is abruptly halted. Shortly after being discharged from the hospital, his health quickly deteriorated, leading to urgent readmission to intensive care. An edema developed in a particularly sensitive area of his skull. The outlook was grim, as the edema's growth threatened to impair his motor functions.

The doctors lived up to their oaths and expertise. Following a five-hour surgery, they placed Alberto in a coma for three weeks. Upon awakening, his healthcare team joyfully informed him that the surgery had been a success. He was out of danger, with no lasting damage from the incident.

The toughest challenge was yet ahead. Rehabilitation was long and grueling for a competitor like him. Contador began walking two months later, and by the end of the year, in December, he was back on the bike.

He greatly missed competition. Eagerly diving back into racing, the rider from Madrid won the fifth stage of the Tour Down Under in January 2005. The ordeal he had endured was harrowing, both mentally and physically. Many riders might not have returned to cycling at all... But he did! More than just returning, he resumed his journey towards becoming a champion.

His team, now Liberty Seguros-Würth, confirmed his participation in his first Tour de France. There, Alberto Contador made his mark with a notable breakaway in the 12th stage, ultimately finishing 31st overall.

True to his nature, he continued to impress at various UCI Pro Tour events. However, his momentum was abruptly halted in late June 2006. His name was mentioned in the Operation Puerto doping case. Though he was cleared of any wrongdoing, he had to "stay in dock" while the investigation was conducted.

When he returned to competition in early August, his results were significantly more impressive. A new chapter of victories, triumphs, and achievements was about to be written.

Recruited by Discovery Channel, the team of the newly retired Lance Armstrong, Contador, nicknamed the Pistolero for his victory salute mimicking firing a gun, would fully leverage the American team's firepower.

Officially a support rider for Levi Leipheimer, Alberto took the 2007 Tour de France into his own hands. He battled Michael Rasmussen, who he couldn't overtake, and was in second place overall.

With the yellow jersey held by Rasmussen, the narrative took a sudden turn. Shocking news hit the headlines: Michael Rasmussen wouldn't start the 17th stage! His team, Rabobank, had fired him for "internal code violations." Just when the story seemed set in stone, the yellow jersey was unexpectedly passed to the Pistolero. He wore it all the way to the Champs-Élysées, even outperforming his team leader, Leipheimer.

With the dissolution of Team Discovery Channel, Contador signed with the Kazakh team Astana. Due to various recent "issues," like the Vinokourov case, the team fell out of favor. Snubbed by some organizers, it wasn't invited to major events, preventing Alberto from defending his title in races like Paris-Nice and the Tour de France. However, Astana surprisingly made it to the Giro and Vuelta.

To keep mentally fresh and maintain team cohesion during a rather dull season, Astana's management urged its riders to excel in any race, regardless of its stakes. The Pistolero heeded the call. He won his first Tour of Italy and soon after, his first Tour of Spain. In his homeland, in front of his people, he became the first Spaniard to win all three Grand Tours and achieve the Giro-Vuelta double in the same year. Unfortunately, he just missed the podium at the Beijing Olympics, finishing fourth in the time trial.

In 2009, the Madrilenian confirmed his dominance by winning the Tour of Algarve and the Tour of the Basque Country. He started the Tour de France, launched in Monaco, wearing the Spanish national time trial champion's jersey. With this title, Alberto proved once more that he could secure victories in long and challenging races. Sharp in the mountains and decisive in time trials, his skill set allowed him to dream of the highest accolades.

At that time, a big name made a comeback, intent on proving he hadn't lost his edge: Lance Armstrong. But could the American really compete with the current best in cycling? Could he replicate his past glories?

To address the cycling world's legitimate questions, Armstrong joined... Astana. He aimed to play a key role in the team. However, the Pistolero was not inclined to relinquish his hard-earned and well-deserved leadership to a comeback star, no matter how illustrious.

Despite internal tensions within the Kazakh team, the Madrilenian clinched his second Tour de France victory. In Paris, the final podium photo spoke volumes. While the young Spaniard beamed triumphantly in his yellow jersey, Lance, on the third step, wore a vacant expression that said it all. Disillusioned, he watched his teammate's success, coming to terms with the fact that while he might lead Astana, it was the Spaniard who was racking up the victories.

Riding the wave of success, the Pistolero continued to shine, winning the Tour of Algarve and Paris-Nice once more. He was the clear favorite for the 2010 Tour de France. And he lived up to his reputation! Battling tooth and nail with Andy Schleck, he won the Grand Boucle for the third time, edging out the Luxembourger by just 31 seconds.

In 2011, he joined Team Saxobank, under the leadership of Bjarne Riis, setting his sights high. The Pistolero aimed to make history by winning all three Grand Tours in a single season. He triumphed at the 2011 Giro, celebrated in Milan's Piazza del Duomo. However, that ended up being his sole Grand Tour victory that season, falling short of his lofty ambition.

Come February 2012, after extensive, twist-filled investigations, Alberto Contador received a two-year suspension from the Court of Arbitration for Sport. The suspension came after a urine sample from the 2010 Tour de France tested positive for Clenbuterol.

This suspension was partly retroactive, allowing for a relatively swift return to competition. Nevertheless, it led to his disqualification from the 2010 Tour and the forfeiture of all his achievements in 2011 and early 2012.

The sanction hit hard, delivering a significant blow to Contador. After serving his suspension, he reentered the competitive scene in early August 2012. Though he missed the Tour de France, he came back fiercely determined for the Vuelta a España.

This Vuelta was unique, taking place entirely in the country's north, with Madrid being the most southern point and the race's finale. The route, featuring ten summit finishes, seemed perfectly suited for Contador, known as one of his generation's premier climbers.

Yet, Contador encountered unexpected challenges. Rivals like Rodríguez, Froome, and Valverde, all eyeing the overall win, strategically worked to neutralize the Madrid native. Contador struggled to assert his dominance and, as the race neared its end, faced the daunting task of needing to perform a miracle to win.

The race heated up by the third stage, which included several climbs. Alejandro Valverde clinched the win in Eibar, snagging the red leader's jersey from his Movistar teammate, Jonathan Castroviejo. However, the dynamics of the race quickly shifted. Anticipated to be challenging and demanding, the Vuelta turned out to be nothing short of spectacular.

On the next day, as Team Sky, led by Chris Froome, made an "echelon", Valverde crashed. Struggling to maintain his lead, he exerted himself on the final to Valdezcaray but failed to catch up.

Joaquim Rodríguez, affectionately nicknamed Purito (Cigarillo), took advantage of the stage's layout, earning the red jersey by the slimmest one-second margin. Froome trailed by a second, and Contador was just five seconds behind, with Valverde falling to fourth, 36 seconds back.

Rodríguez's lead was minimal, but he ended the day as the biggest beneficiary. He committed himself to defending this slender lead, winning the uphill finish in Jaca during stage 6.

In Andorra, atop the Gallina summit, he dueled with Valverde, who outsprinted him to win stage eight. Alberto Contador was close behind, keeping a watchful eye on the general classification. Meanwhile, Froome faltered, losing approximately 20 seconds.

Rodríguez was in top form that year, handling the climbs with relative ease and securing another second-place finish on stage 9. This strong showing at the Alto de Montjuich further cemented his position at the top. Through time bonuses and savvy racing, Rodríguez built and maintained a lead that steadily grew, keeping him roughly a minute ahead of his closest competitors.

The 11th stage, a 40 km time trial from Cambados to Pontevedra, marked a significant turning point. As the Vuelta entered its second half, the intensity of the competition ratcheted up. The battle grew increasingly fierce day by day, with each rider launching multiple attacks against their rivals, hoping to gradually wear them down for the final victory.

Swedish cyclist Fredrik Kessiakoff caused a stir by winning this time trial, beating Contador by 17 seconds. Froome had an off day, finishing third in the stage but trailing Kessiakoff by over 40 seconds. Purito, however, clung on tenaciously. Although he gave up a minute to Contador in the general classification, he kept the red jersey by a mere second! Once again, he led the Vuelta, demonstrating his determination and hard work. Joaquim, a climber of modest stature, won the hearts of fans and cycling enthusiasts with his perseverance and courage, earning widespread support and encouragement along the way. This unexpected backing gave Purito an essential boost towards victory in Madrid. Day after day, he managed to keep his red jersey, even through the most challenging stages.

Yet, the journey to Spain's capital was still long. Starting with the 14th stage, the peloton faced the toughest climbs. Entering the high mountains of the Asturias marked a new phase of the race.

The high altitudes sharpened Alberto Contador's appetite for victory. As the days passed, he knew his window to take the leader's jersey was closing fast.

The Pistolero then adopted a much more aggressive stance. With no other option, he had to seize the initiative. During the 14th stage, he launched relentless attacks on Rodríguez. But Purito held firm, not only resisting but also beating Contador in a sprint finish at Puerto de Ancares. Thanks to the time bonuses, he extended his lead to 22 seconds.

The following day, Rodríguez, Contador, and Valverde neutralized each other, while Froome, continuing to struggle, dropped another 35 seconds. The next stage promised much more action.

The climb to the daunting Cuitu Negru summit, the finish of stage 16, was like an ascent through hell. With no shade in sight, the riders tackled slopes reaching 25% gradients in the final kilometers, where even the most agile appeared to be moving in slow motion.

The day's victory went to Dario Cataldo, who broke away solo. The main contenders were too busy settling scores among themselves.

While Cataldo led alone, Rodríguez, Valverde, and Contador briefly formed a chasing group. However, their real battle wasn't with Cataldo but with each other. Like a true bullfighter, the Pistolero continuously attacked, prodding and pestering his rivals, trying to break them.

Valverde was the first to fall behind after a ferocious surge from Alberto. But Joaquim kept pace, even launching a counterattack in the last kilometer! The two Spaniards engaged in a fierce duel on the final steep ramp, a narrow path with a 23% gradient.

Rodríguez showed why he was a contender, managing to gain a few seconds on Contador in the final stretch. The resistance from the Katusha rider was nothing short of heroic.

The intense battle for first place was exhausting. Following the finish at Ciutu Negru, a much-needed rest day was scheduled. With just a few stages left before reaching Madrid, the outcome was far from decided, especially as the contenders, led by Alberto Contador, became increasingly assertive.

The leader of SaxoBank found himself in a tricky situation. He had managed to put some distance between himself, Valverde, and Froome in the general classification. Feeling still fresh and ready to launch an attack at any moment, as was his signature, he was poised for action. However, Rodríguez had proven his mettle. Boosted by the enthusiasm he was generating, dislodging him would be a formidable task. With relentless determination, Purito was carving a path to victory. To neutralize him, Contador needed to outsmart him on more than just physical strength...

During the rest day, the Pistolero's mind was racing. By the next day, before the start of the 17th stage, he arrived at the briefing with a strategy—a real trap for the red jersey...

Observing that most Katusha riders, Rodríguez included, hadn't left their hotel the previous day, Contador spotted an opportunity. In multi-week races, it's crucial to keep the body, especially the legs, active during rest days to maintain conditioning. Conversely, suddenly stopping all pedaling for over 24 hours can have detrimental effects on the body.

Alberto, who had kept his legs moving the day before, bet on a collective Katusha burnout during the race. He put all his chips on this gamble. To complicate matters for the Russian team, he counted on his teammates. Together, they were the linchpin of his elaborate trap. The instructions were clear; it was now or never.

The stage from Santander to Fuente Dé started without notable difficulties. However, from kilometer 118, the challenge would steadily increase, with the grunts of Ozalba and La Hoz, culminating in the finish at Fuente Dé.

Teams like Rabobank, Astana, Sky, and Movistar pulled the bunch, setting a brisk pace to preempt any breakaway attempts.

This approach worked initially. Every attack was quickly neutralized. But around kilometer 80, a group of eleven riders broke away, gaining ground on the peloton as a chase group formed behind them. The two groups merged en route to La Hoz.

This breakaway was more significant than it appeared. Bruno Pires, Jesús Hernández, and Sérgio Paulinho, all from Saxobank, made it into the chase group, their positioning far from coincidental. It was all part of the plan...

As his teammates moved to the front, Contador sprung into action, leaving the peloton behind as he tackled La Hoz alone. With the finish over 50 km away, was this move madness? The risk was enormous, and initially, it seemed unrewarded.

Despite his efforts, he crested La Hoz with only a slim lead over the peloton. Few would have bet on Contador then. Rodríguez, believing he had nothing to worry about, stayed his course.

Rodríguez and Valverde's indifference—both having stayed "warm" in the peloton—played right into Saxobank's hands, allowing them to reveal their strategy.

As the lead group slowed, Contador gradually closed the gap, exerting significant effort. Once he made the connection, the Saxobank delegation at the front prepared for battle. Led by the heroic efforts of Pires, Hernández, and Paulinho, Contador virtually seized the yellow jersey on the descent of La Hoz.

Purito, who had hoped to make a comeback in the descent, didn't realize the extent of his predicament until it was too late. Attempting a counterattack at the start of the climb towards Fuente Dé, he found himself with seven other riders breaking away. However, Rodríguez ended up with only Losada for support, forced to pace a group of leeches unwilling to work with him. Meanwhile, Team Saxobank maintained its dominance. With 25 km to go, Rodríguez's group trailed by 51 seconds. But as they plunged into a steep valley, as if cleaved from rock with an axe, Alberto's support began to wane one by one. Having exhausted themselves, his teammates left their leader to fend for himself.

Now leading the race, he was joined by the amiable Paolo Tiralongo. Racing for Astana, Tiralongo had been Contador's teammate and, in a nod to their shared history and undiminished friendship, unexpectedly took up the mantle to aid his former leader. Their teamwork was seamless, their efforts harmoniously effective. Approaching the final climb, 16 km from the finish, Contador had secured a 2-minute lead. Three kilometers later, the "Pistolero" made his decisive move, leaving Tiralongo, throwing shapes, behind.

For Rodríguez, the situation deteriorated further. With Losada spent from his efforts, Purito was left to spearhead the chase alone, while Valverde skulked behind, merely drafting. Purito resembled the captain of a sinking ship, overlooked by an indifferent crew. The pressure on the red jersey was immense; he was close to breaking.

13 kilometers from the summit, Valverde chose his moment to strike, delivering a fatal blow to Rodríguez. Leading his group, Valverde surged, effectively distancing himself from Contador's allies. Free from contention, Alejandro pressed on.

Initially, Rodríguez managed to keep pace. But as the road widened, Valverde accelerated again, leaving Purito behind. The Catalan blew up. Earlier, he had envisioned cooperation from his breakaway companions, but aside from Losada, none supported him. Worn out and abandoned by a goal-oriented Valverde, Rodríguez faced a grim realization.

Falling behind under Valverde's acceleration meant more than just losing the stage; Rodríguez was forced to concede his leadership to Contador, effectively ending his hopes for the overall victory.

The Movistar team rider aimed to create the largest possible gap between himself and Christopher Froome, who was closely trailing him in the standings. He explained after the stage, "When Contador launched his attack, I stuck to Purito's wheel. Joaquim and I were racing different races. My focus was on gaining as much distance on Froome as possible." Valverde went to great lengths to bridge the gap with Quintana, who had found himself stranded in no-man's land after the earlier breakaway fell apart. Then, the two of them began the chase together because Alejandro still had a shot at the stage win. Soon, they were joined by another teammate, Beñat Intxausti, who was also caught in between.

For Contador, the final kilometers were a solo ordeal. Alone and battling fatigue, he persevered. His pedaling was automatic, his expression stoic. With 5 km remaining, his lead had shrunk to 1'02, despite his efforts. Valverde's teammates from Murcia, motivated and coordinated, were putting in a notable effort, fueling their belief in a stage victory for their leader.

Charged with energy, the Movistar trio kept eating into the race leader's advantage. Contador, tapping into his last reserves in a final stand against the agony, upped his pedaling cadence. As he emerged from the last curve before the finish line, he surged, only to find Valverde, having made a remarkable comeback, was just a hundred meters back.

This slim lead, mere seconds at best, was enough for Contador to eye his redemption. His long battle with the Court of Arbitration for Sport ended with a harsh penalty. Today, the rider from Madrid was eager to erase the memory of that ruling he considered unjust. Six months of suspension and being stripped of his last two Grand Tour victories was a bitter pill to swallow.

In a display of resilience that few possess, Contador signaled his return to the top tier of cycling. He crossed the finish line with fists pumping towards the sky, accompanied by a raw shout of victory. He had turned the tide of an uncertain Vuelta in his favor, in one of the most fiercely contested editions.

In the general classification, Valverde, despite his amazing rally, finished second, 1'52" behind. Rodríguez, the "accursed," after a similar loss in the Giro d'Italia months before, was third, 2'28" back. While Contador's performance was spectacular, the heart goes out to the unlucky yet brave Purito. Such is the fate of the vanquished.

The final standings would not change. In Madrid, Valverde clinched second place, 1'16" behind, and Rodríguez secured third, 1'37" behind. Standing on the podium, the disappointment was evident in the eyes of the Katusha rider, who would never claim a Grand Tour victory.

Contrary to Purito's fate, Alberto Contador's career would be adorned with further major triumphs. He won the Vuelta a España again in 2014 and claimed the pink jersey in the 2015 Giro.

In 2017, as his career dawned, he offered the Vuelta one last stage victory, achieved with flair, before retiring from professional cycling for good.

On the Grand Tour roads, Alberto Contador was unmatched. A relentless attacker and a natural competitor, he never conceded defeat. Powered by his fighter's instinct, his dramatic victories were driven by one thing: the relentless desire to spearhead the offensive.

Printed in Great Britain
by Amazon